GRAFFITI COLORING BOOK

BELONGS TO:

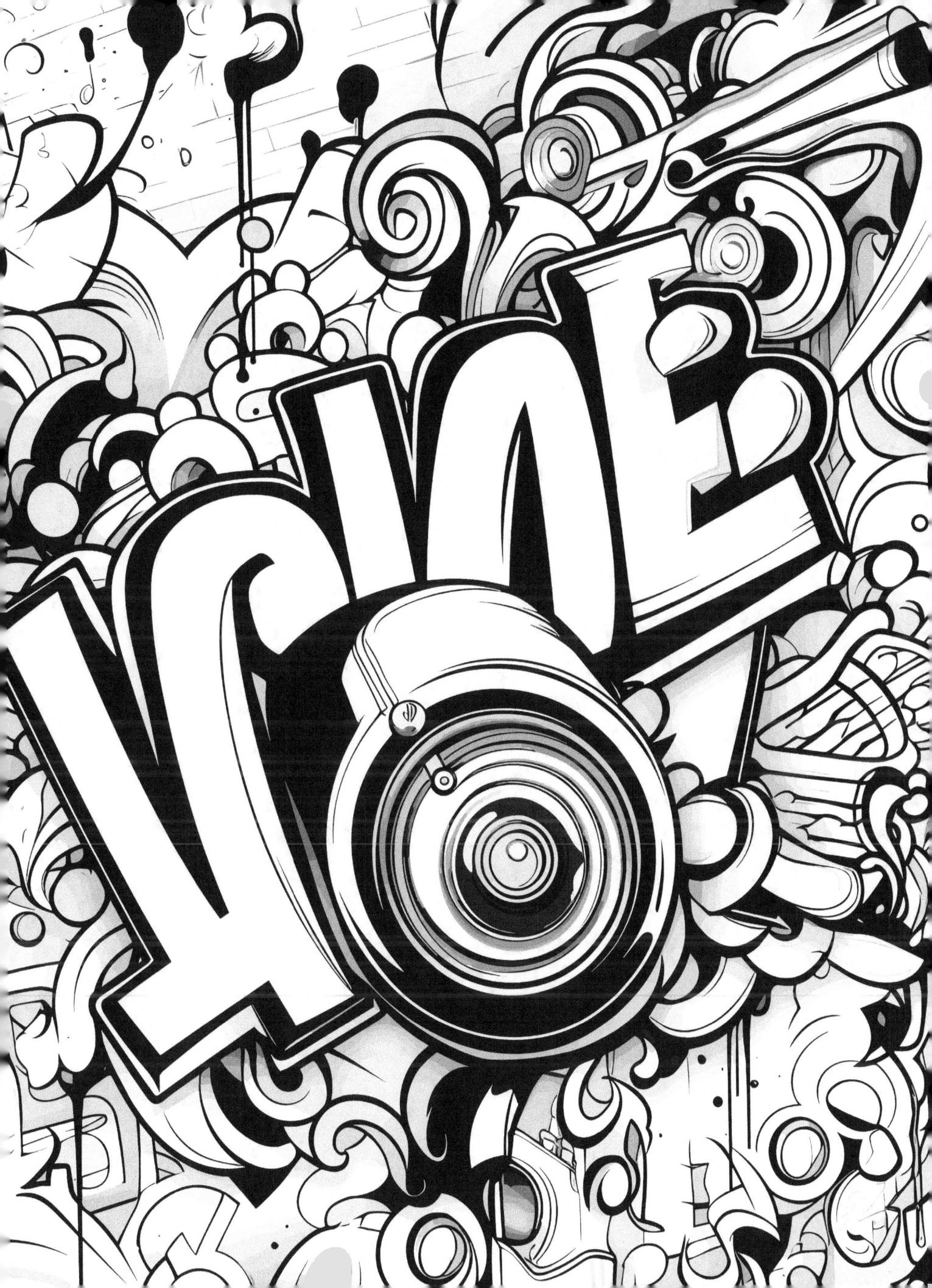

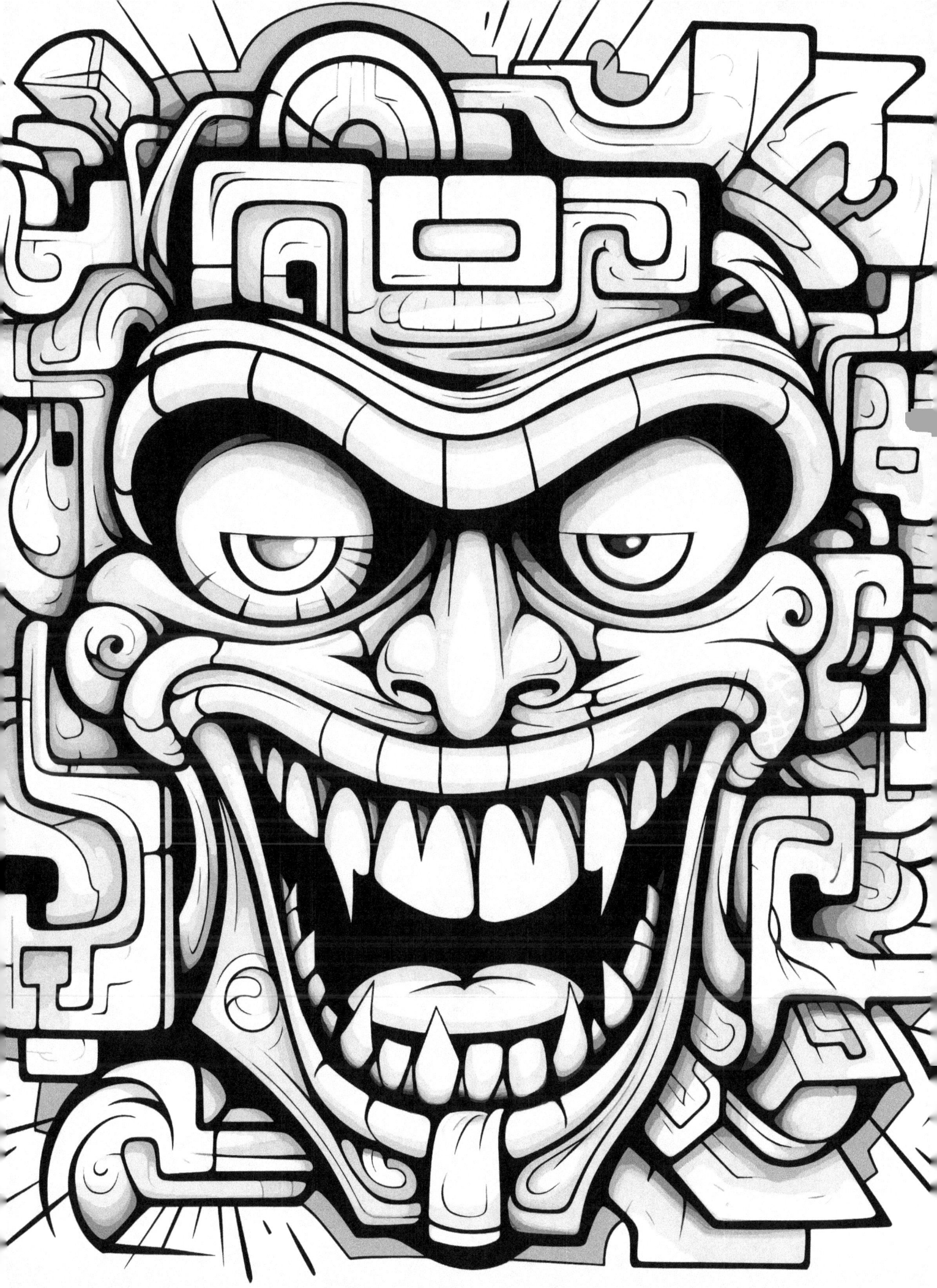

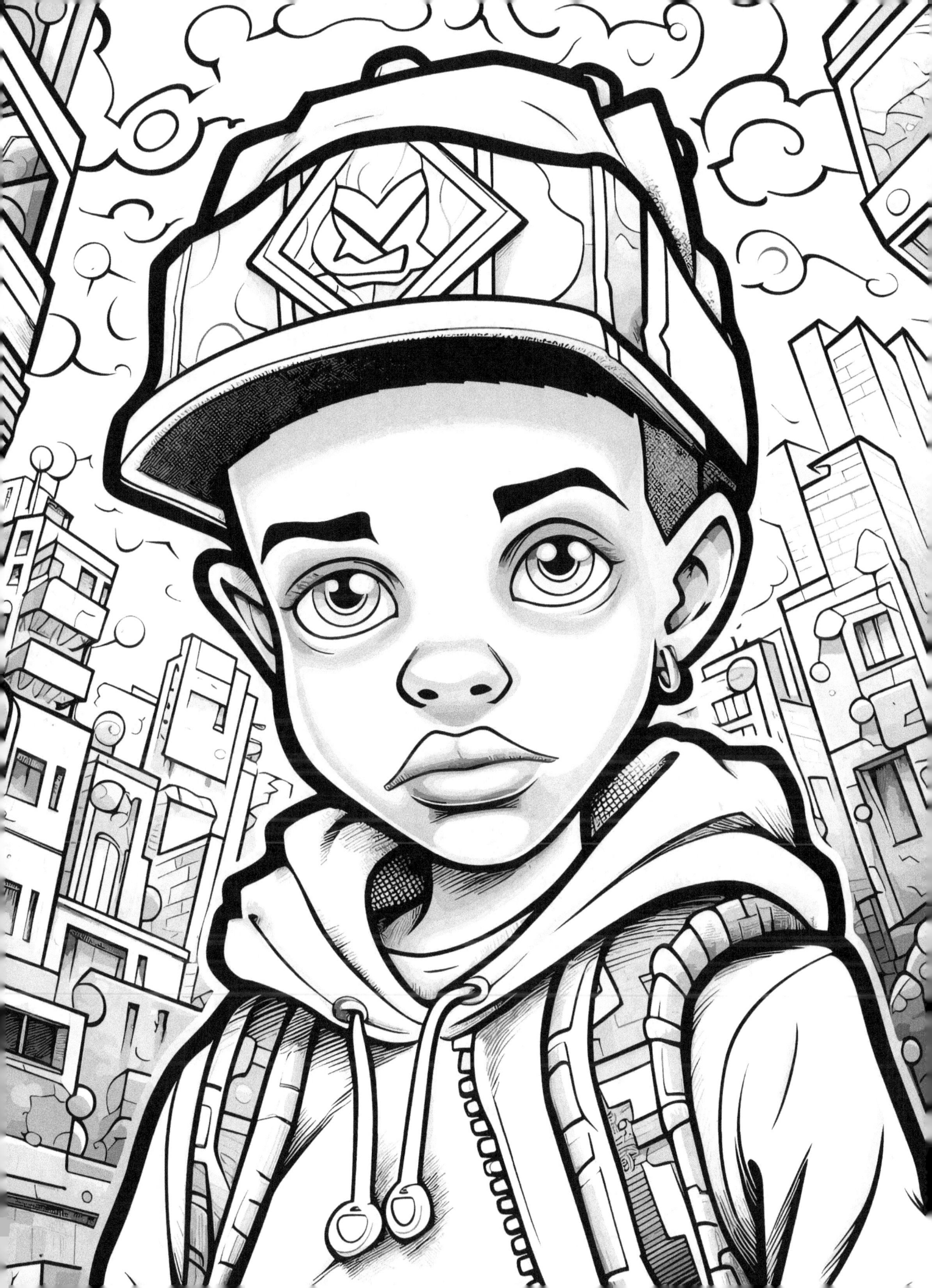

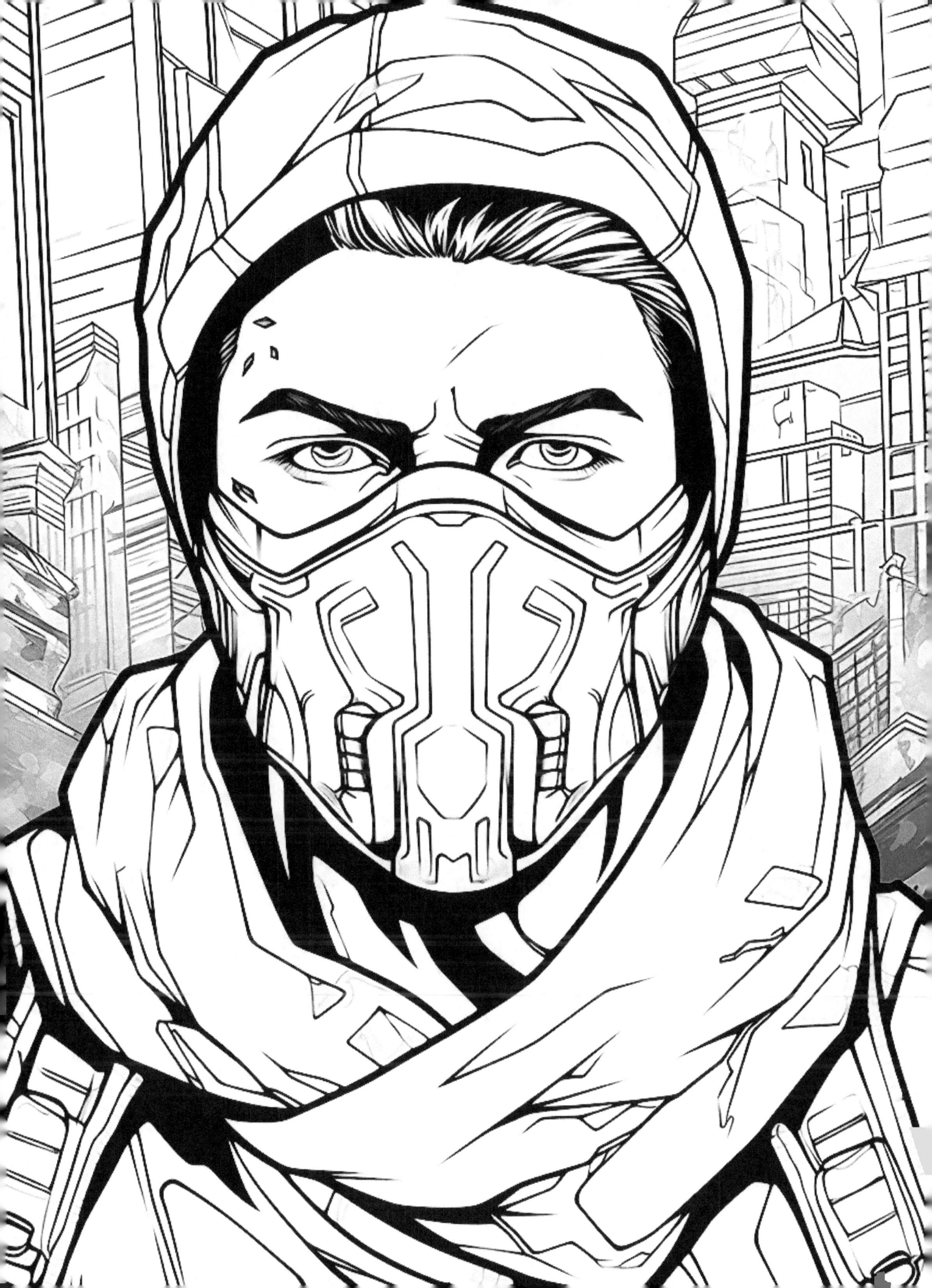

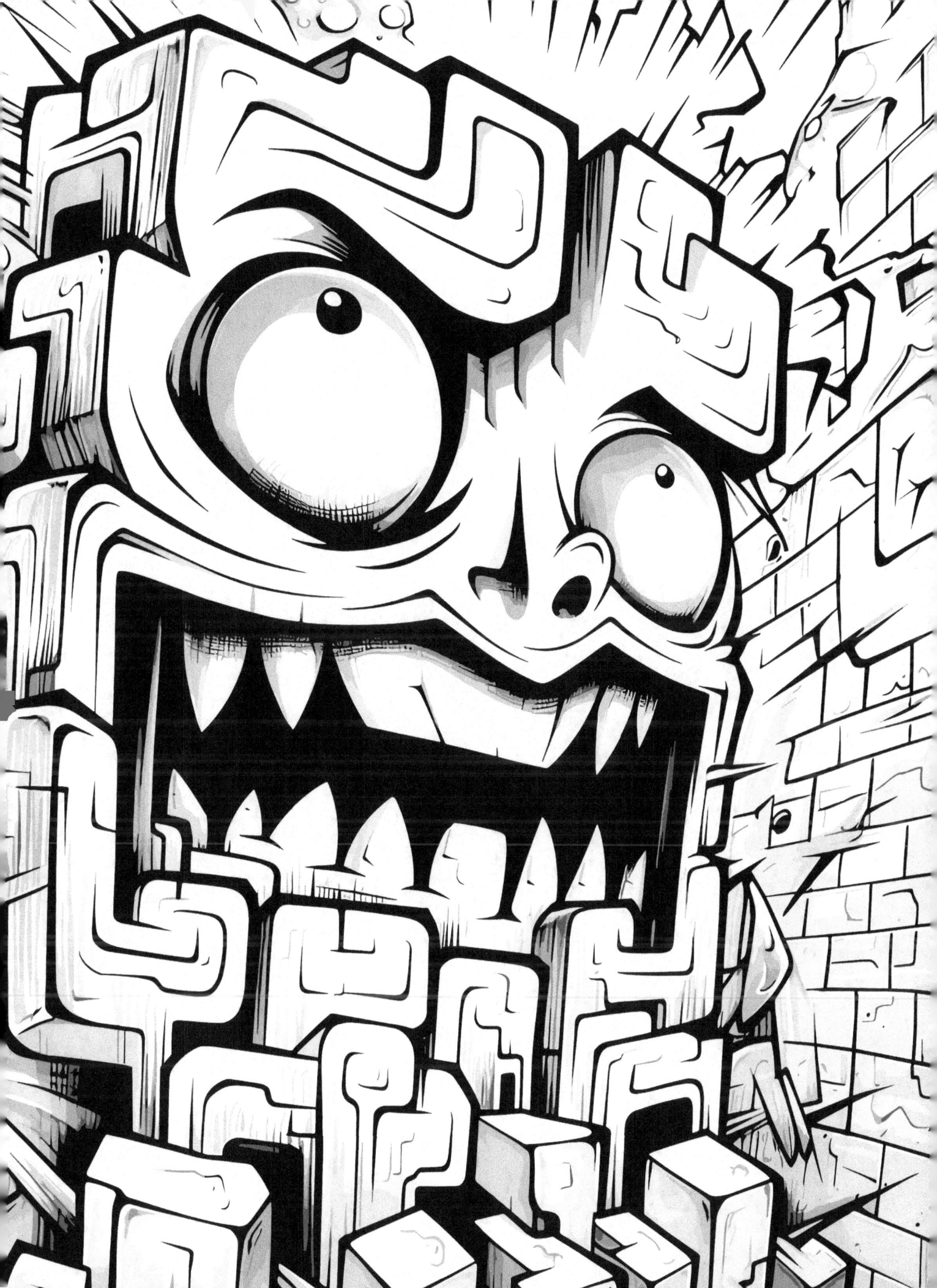

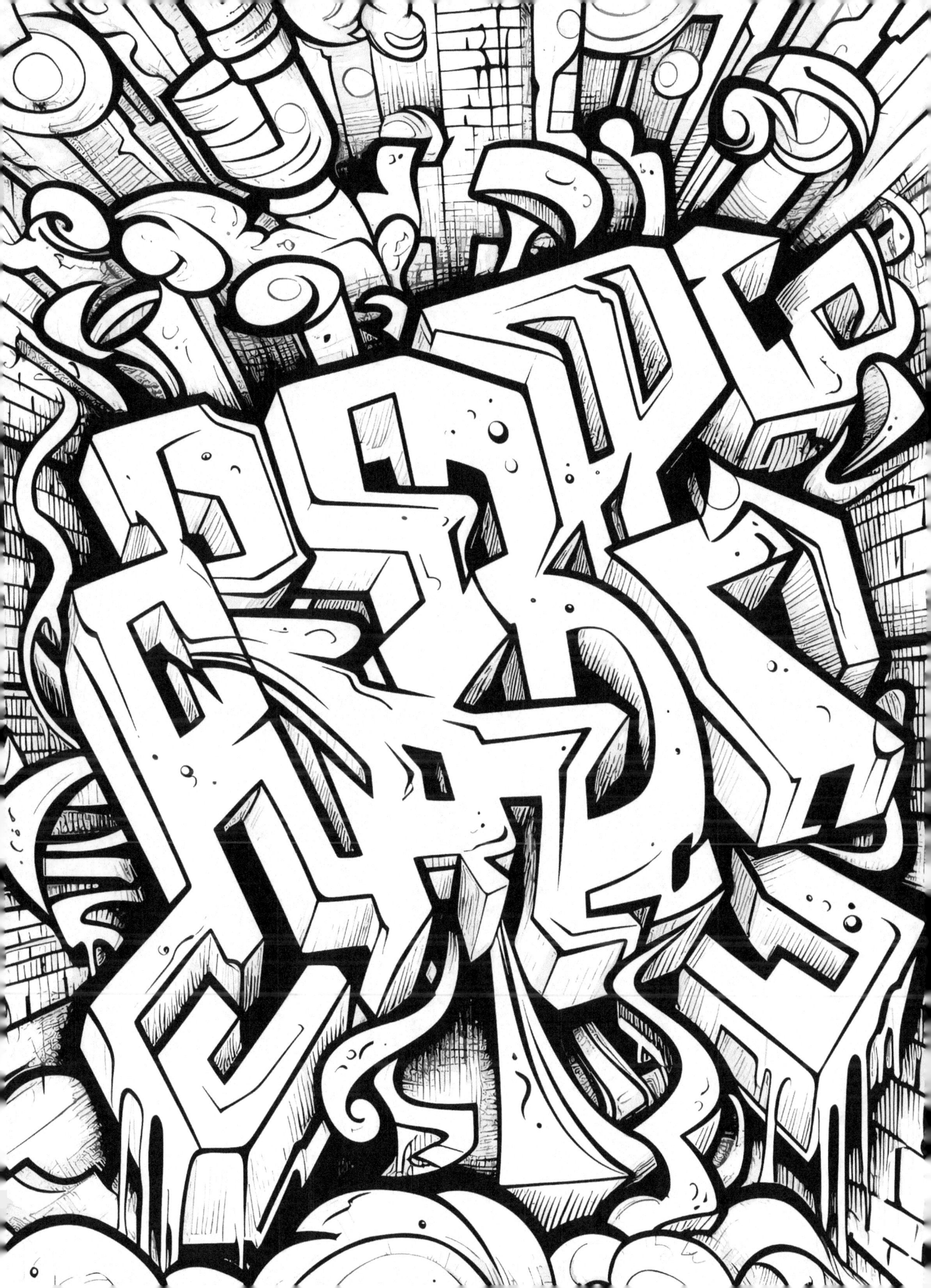

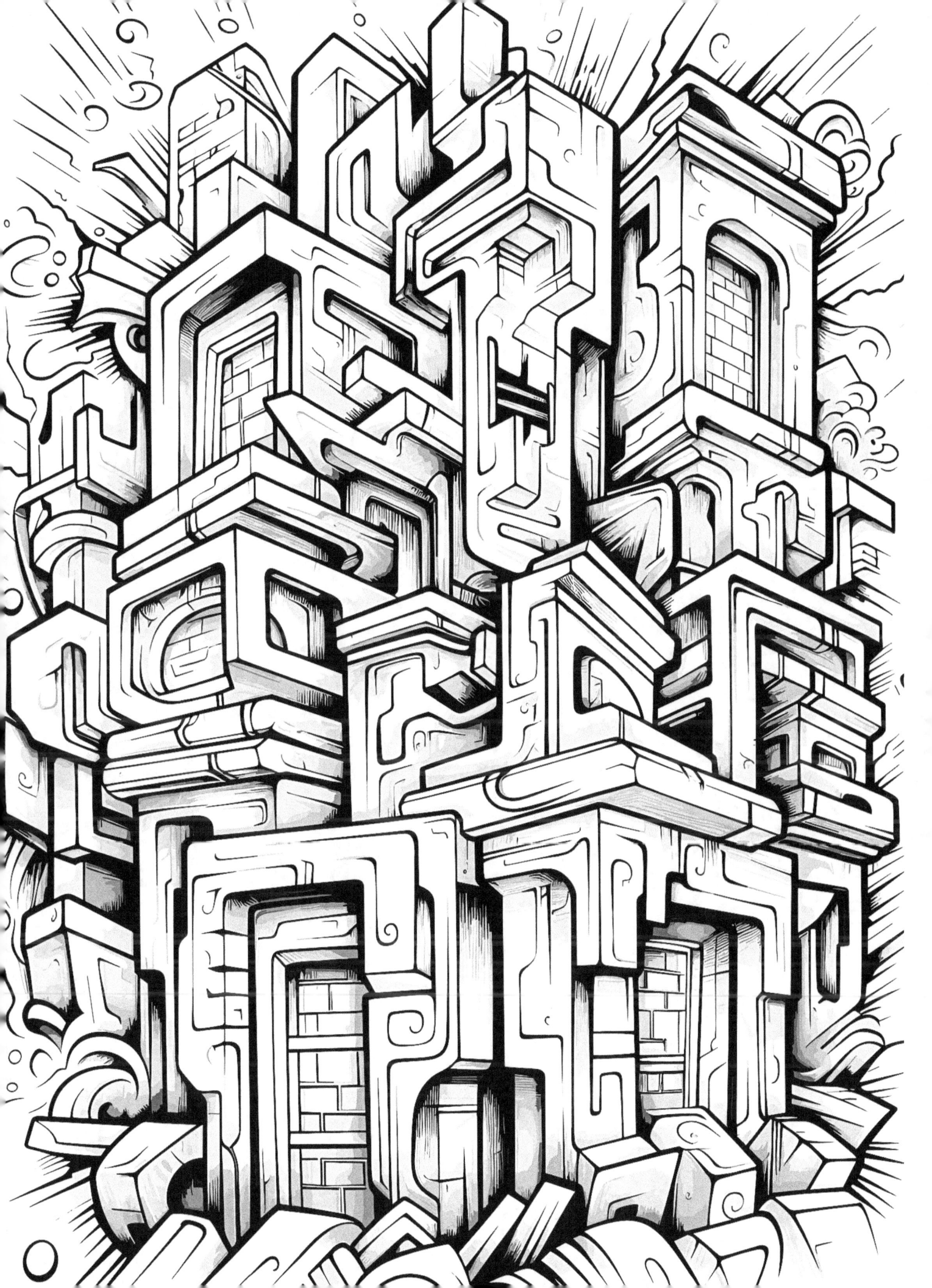

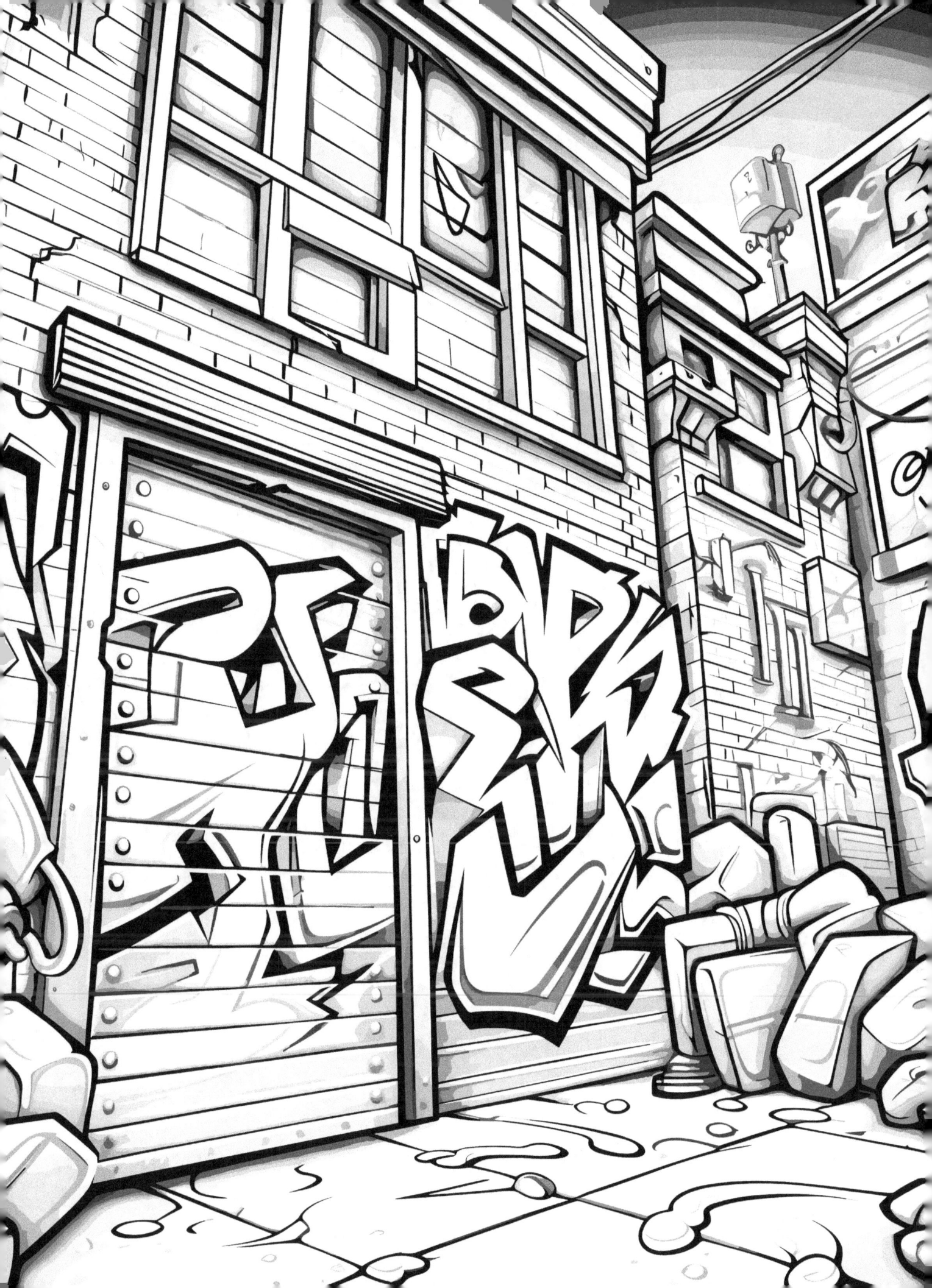

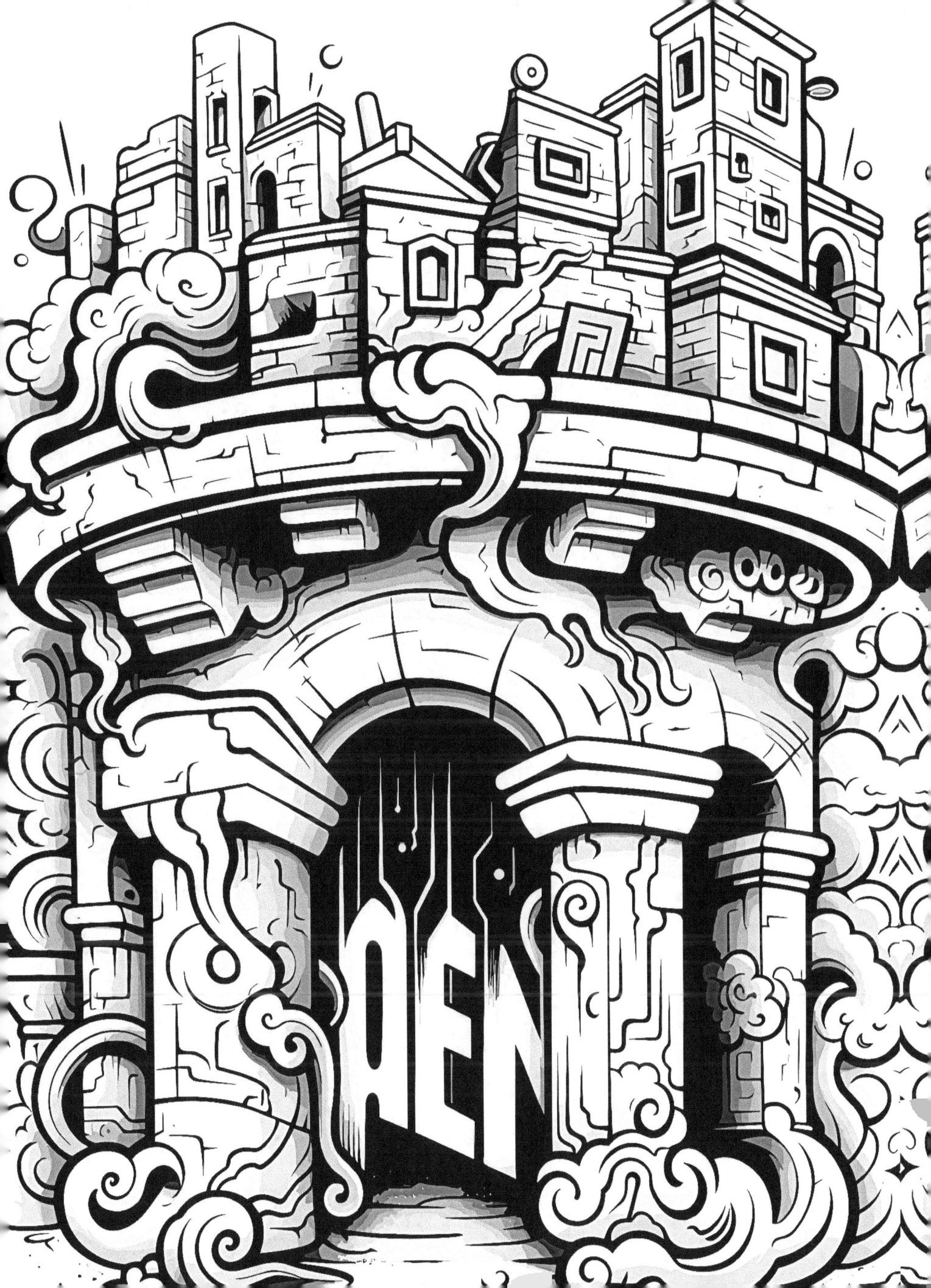

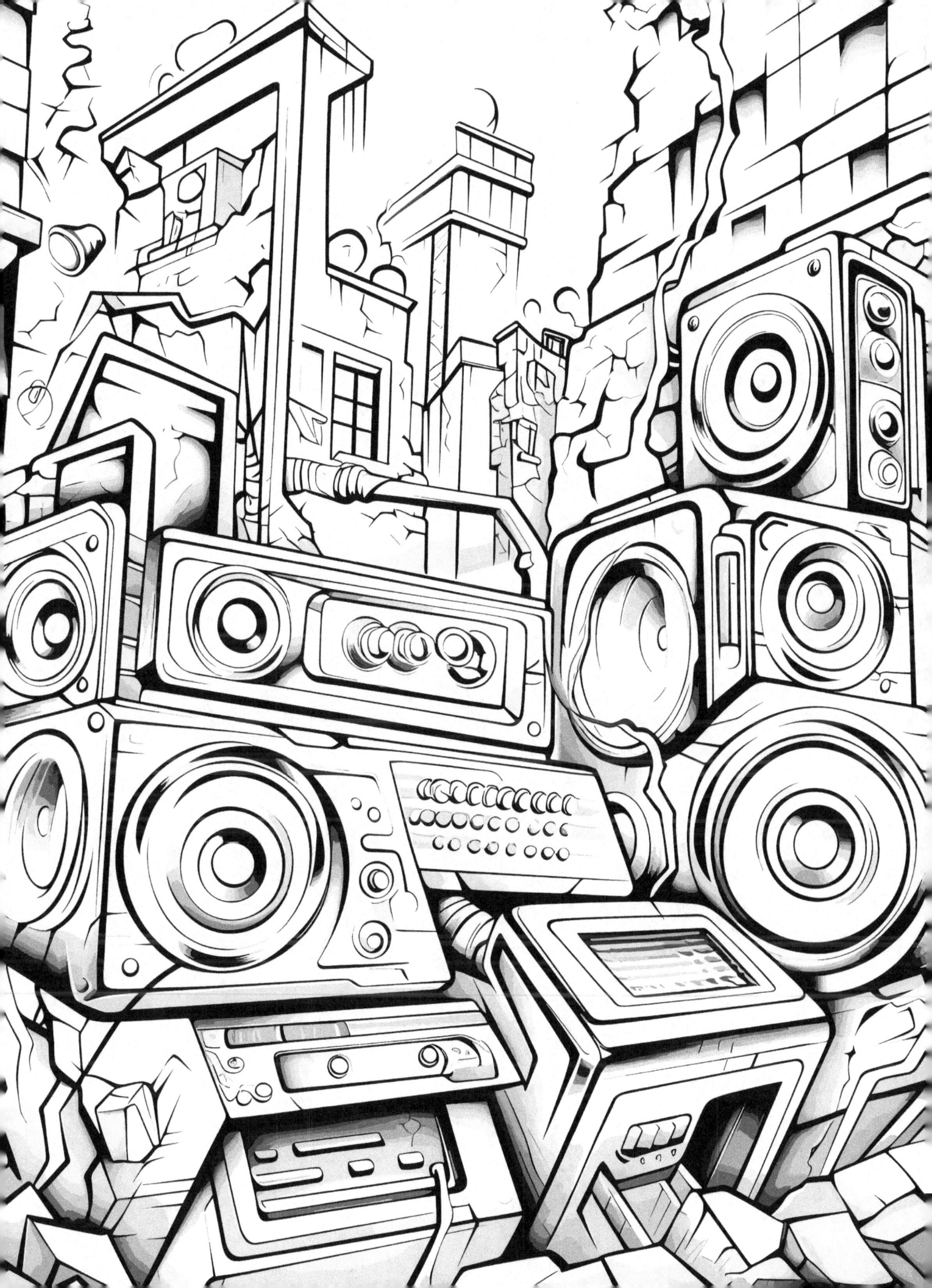

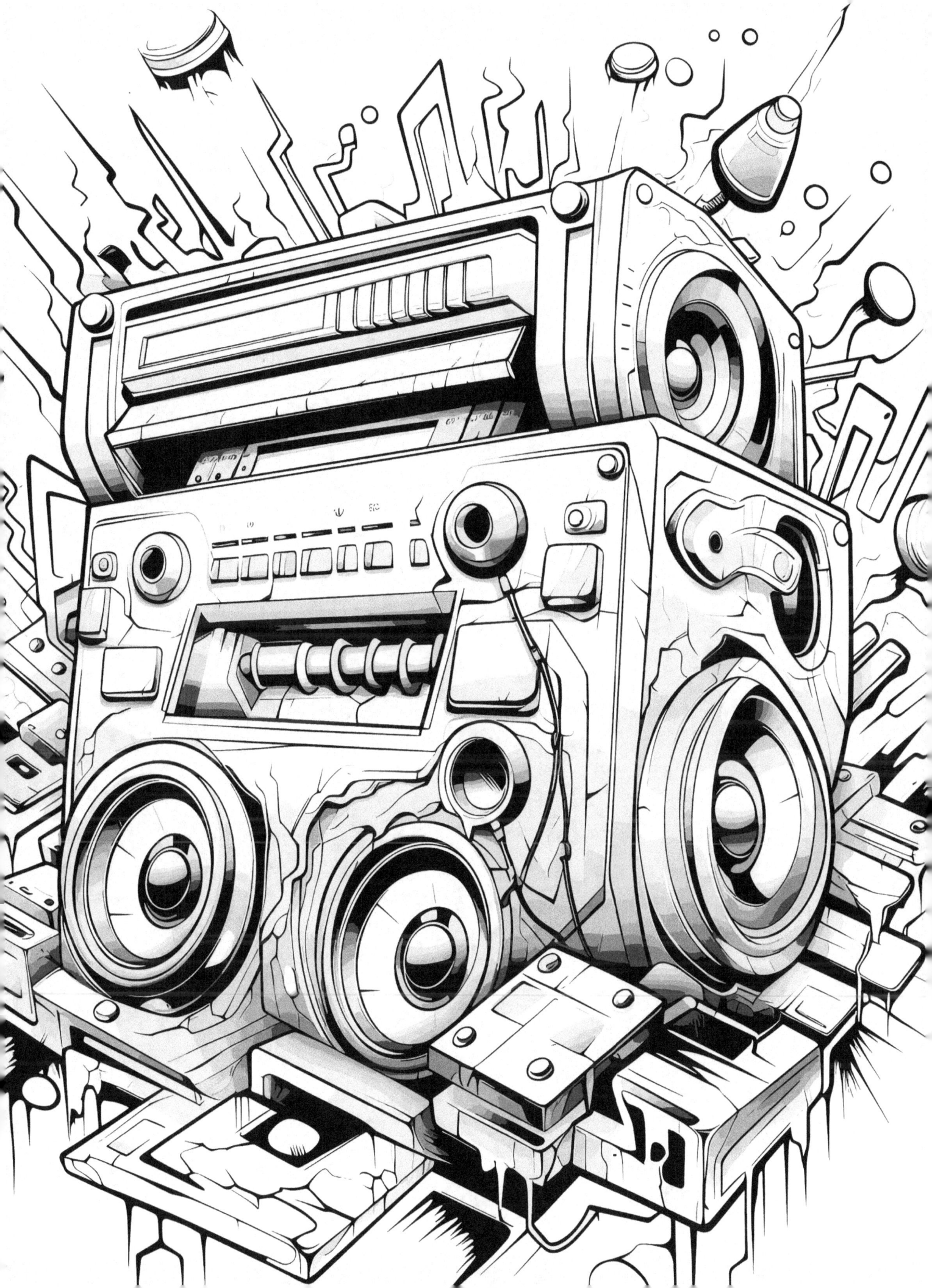

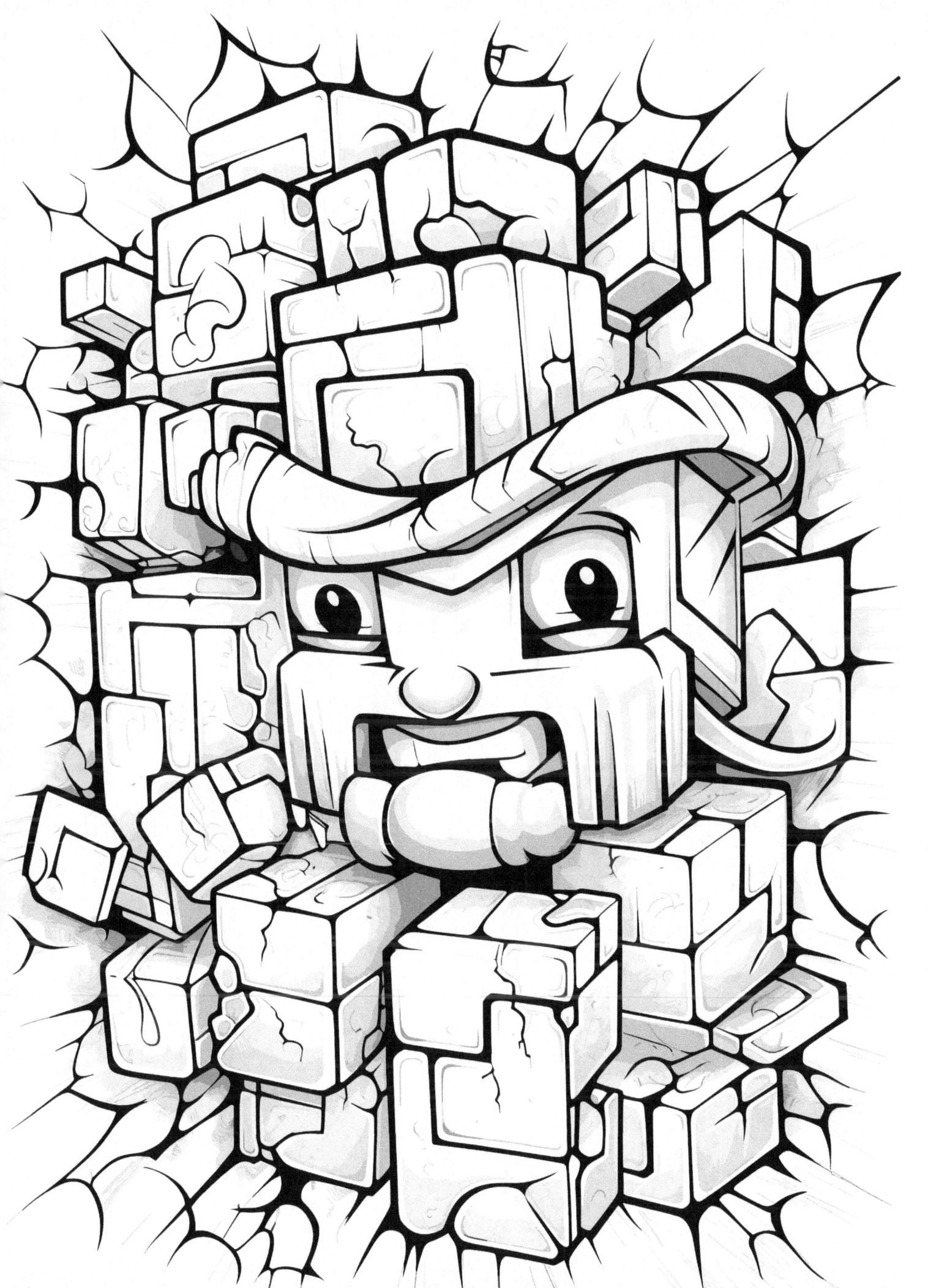

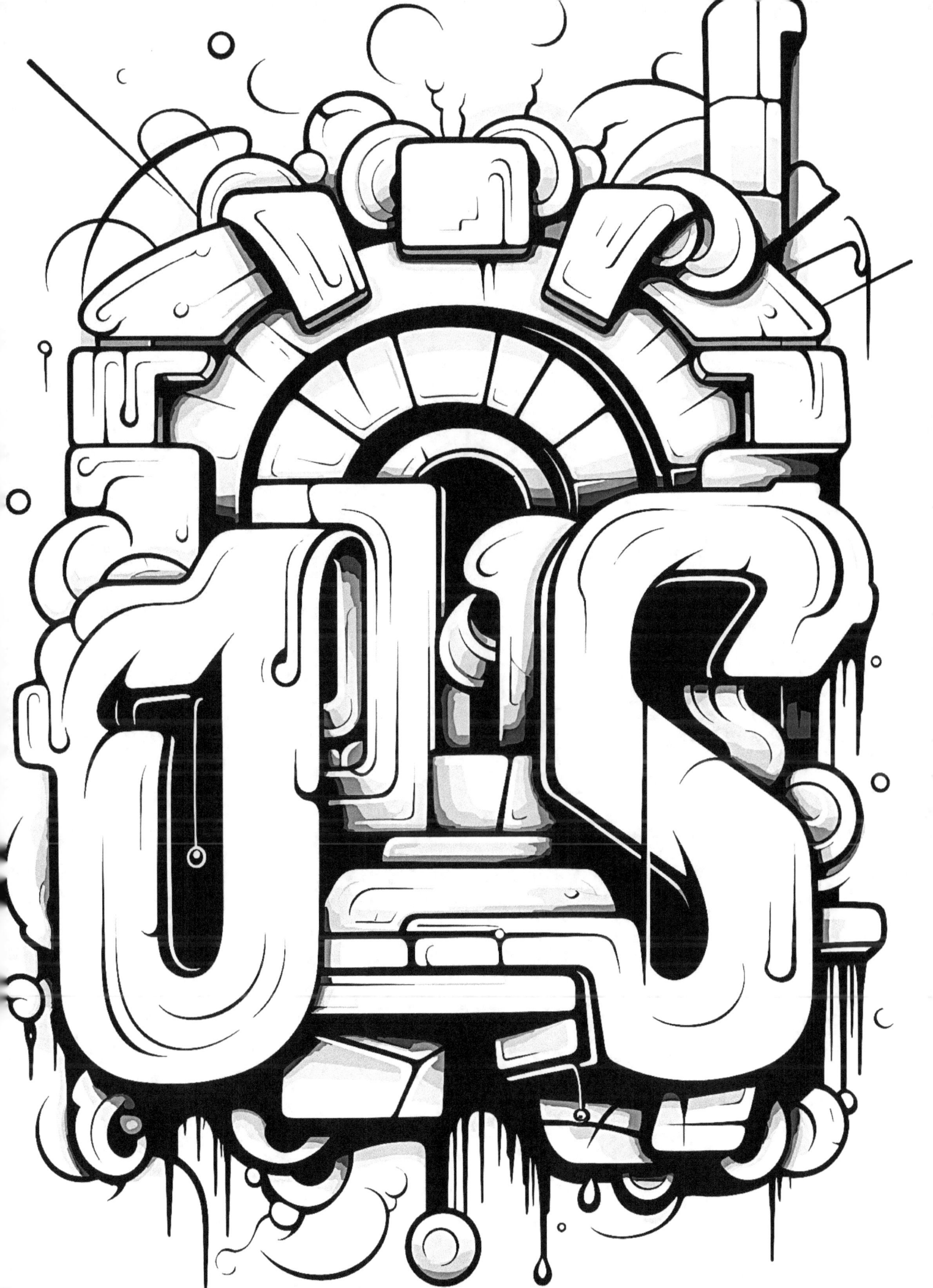

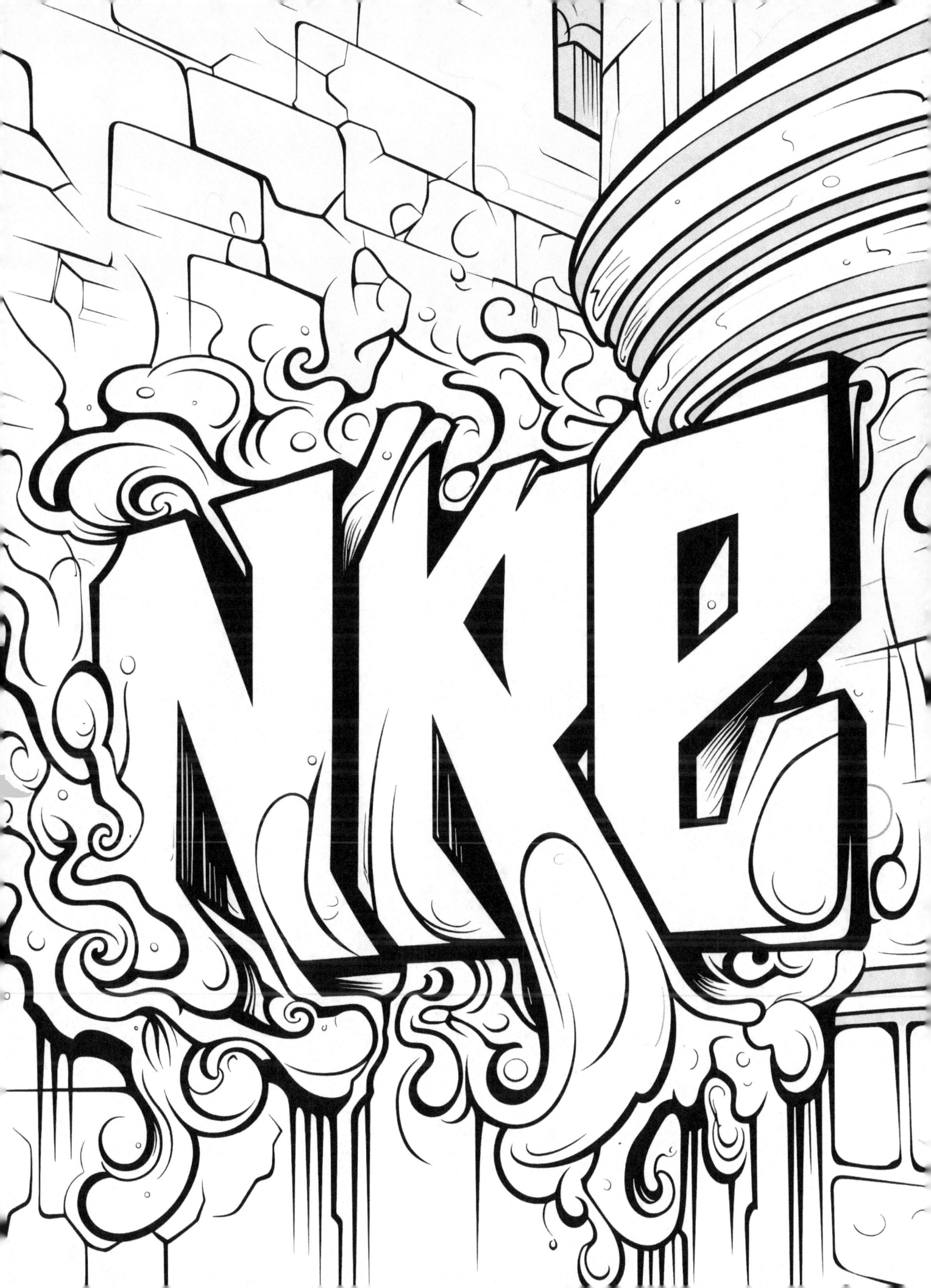

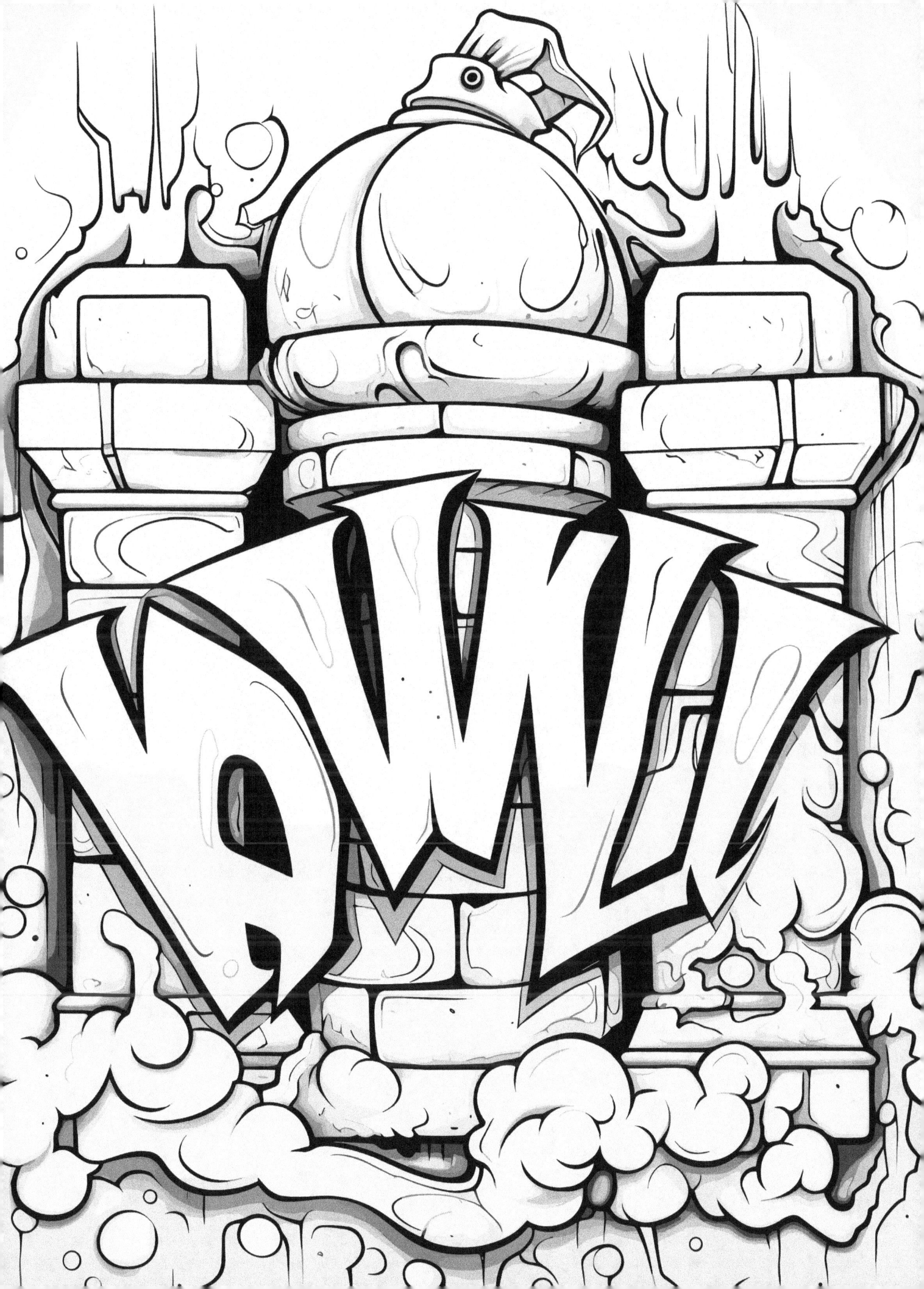

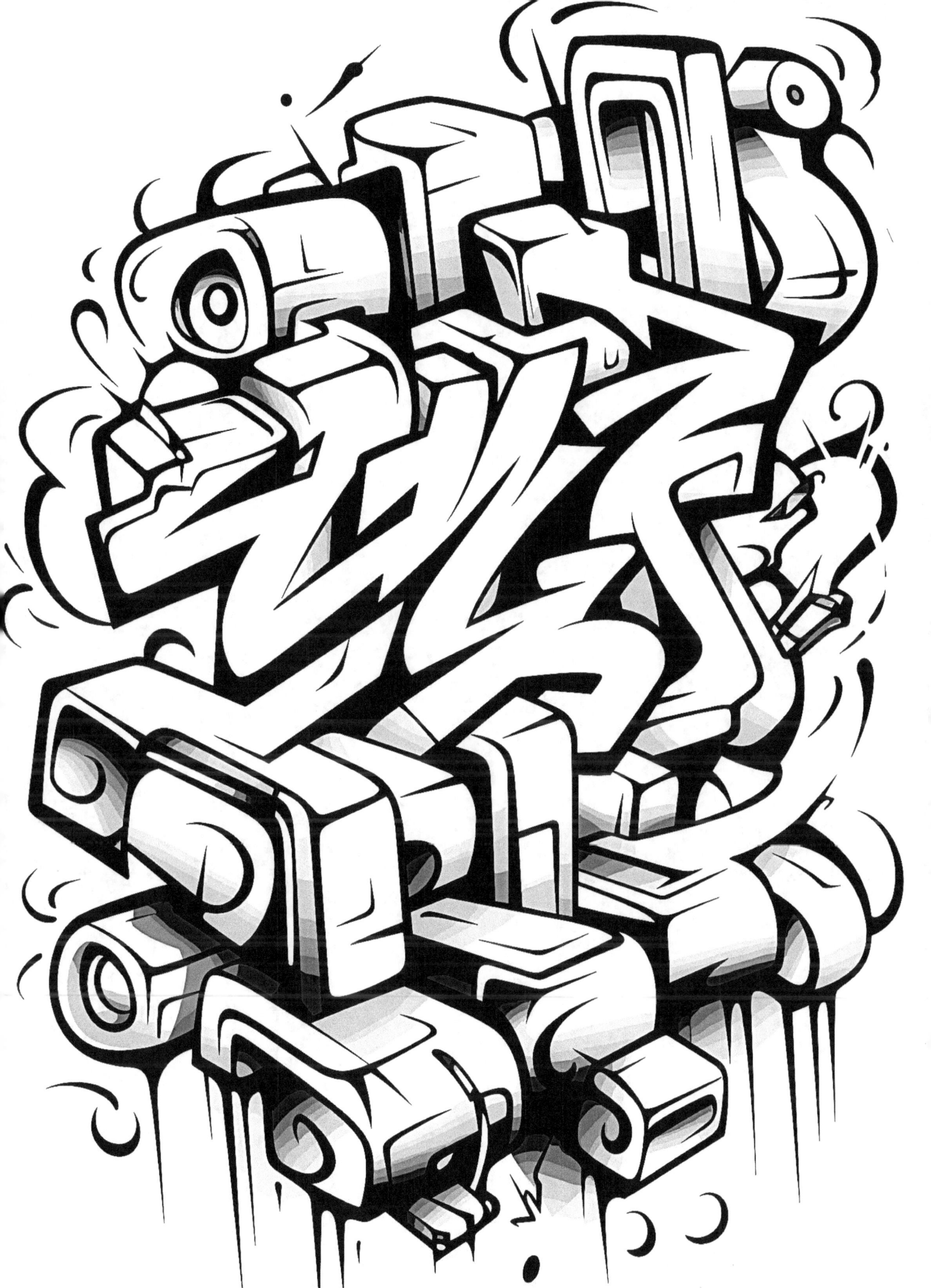

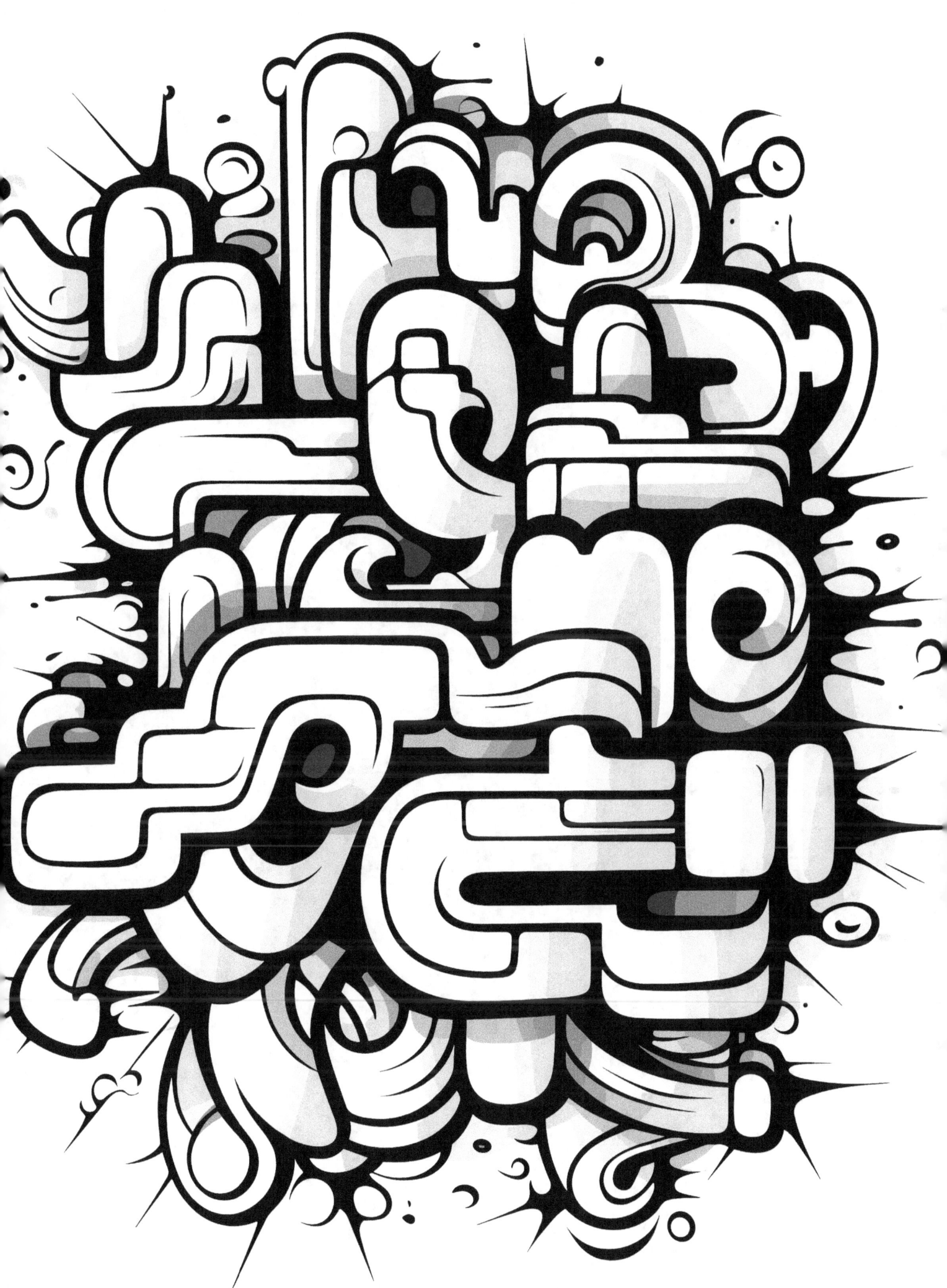

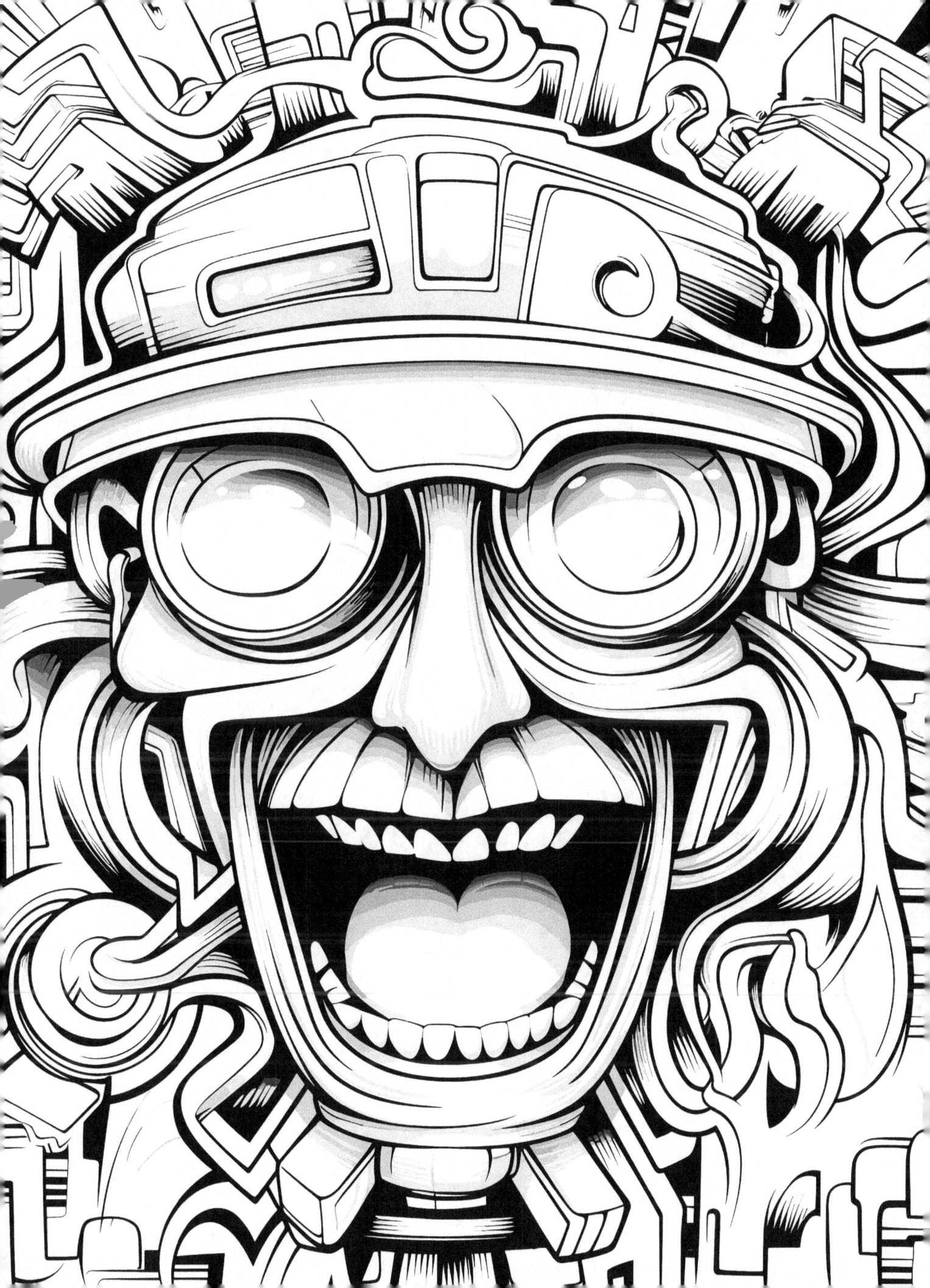

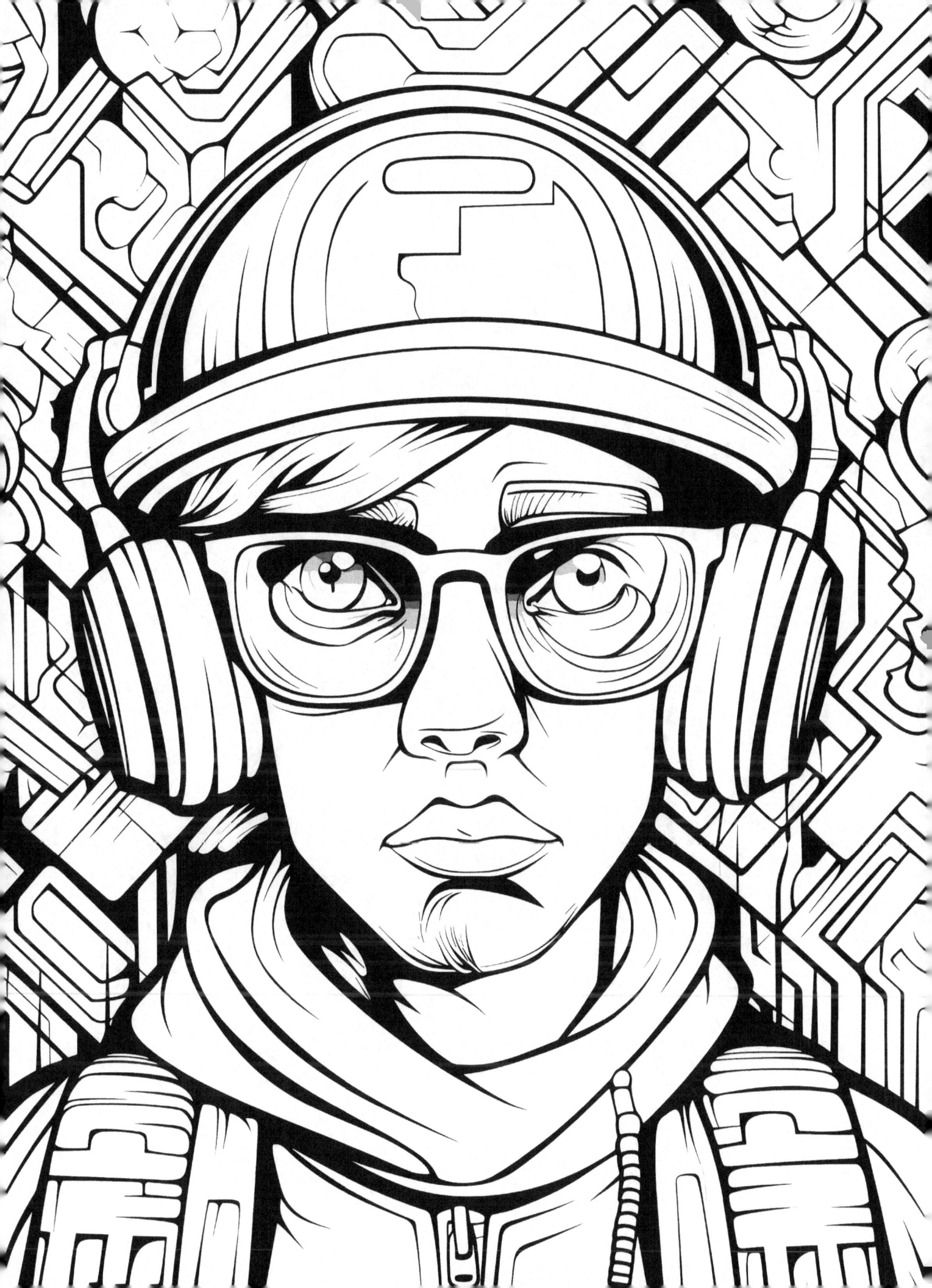

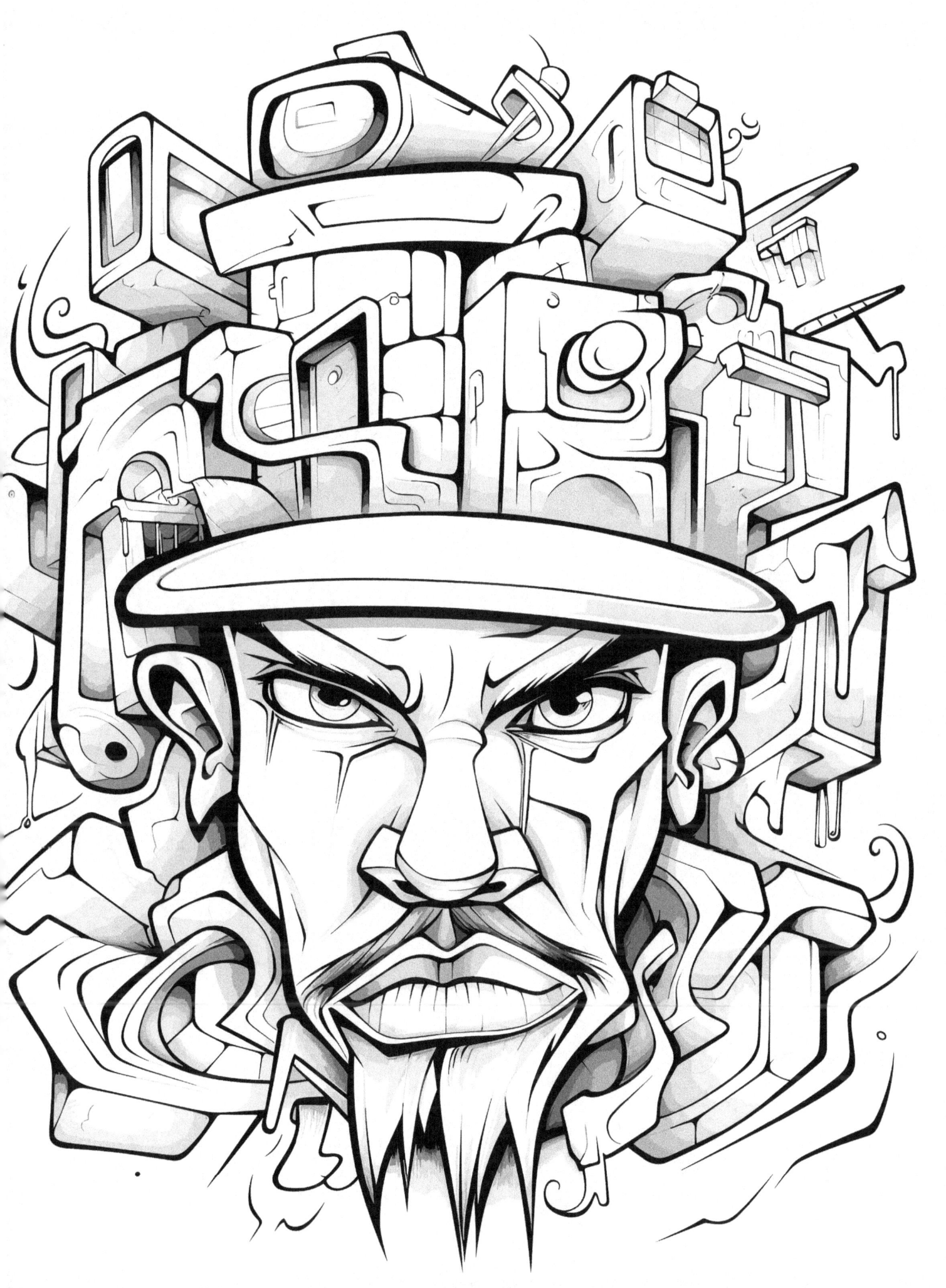

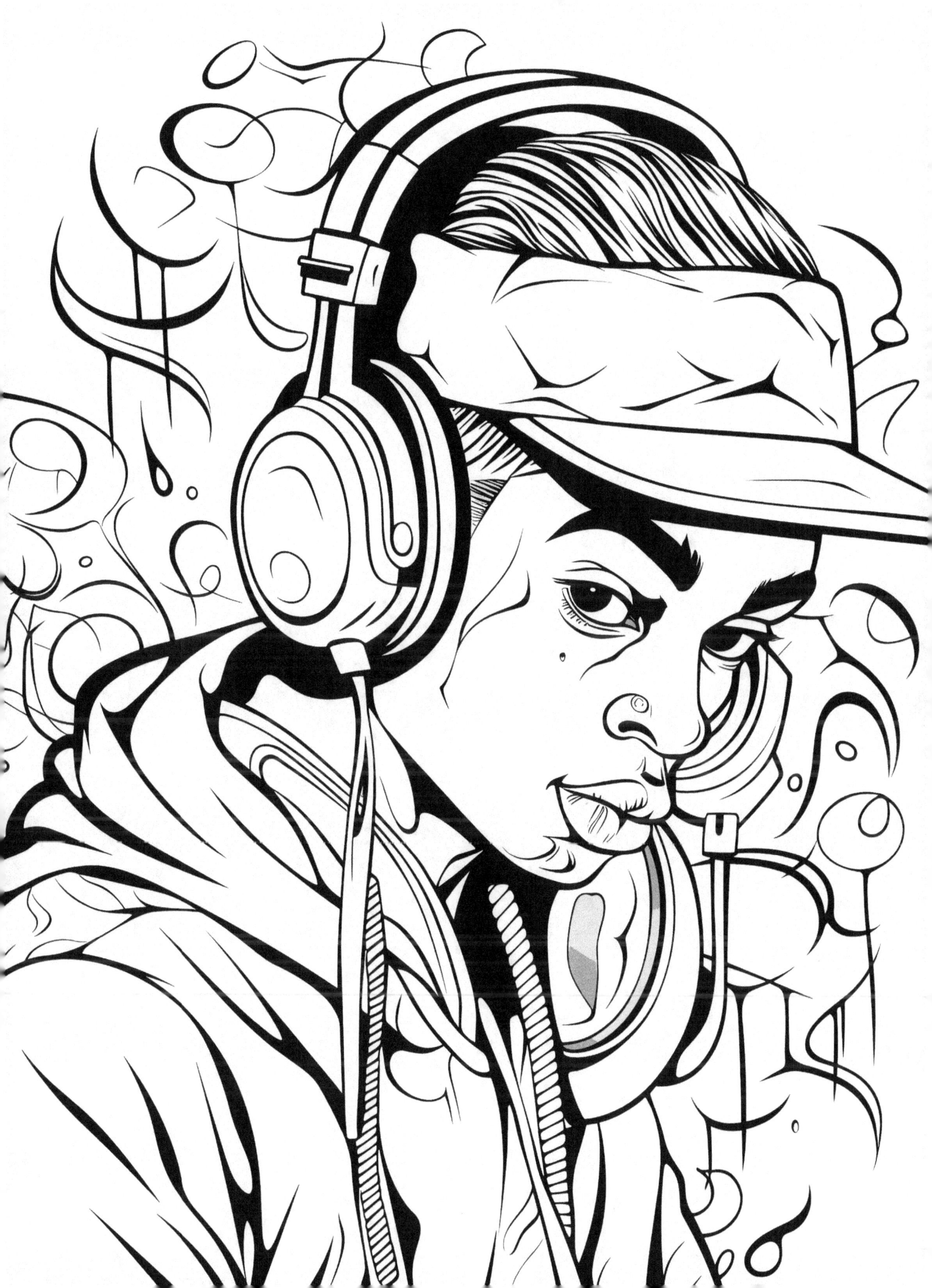

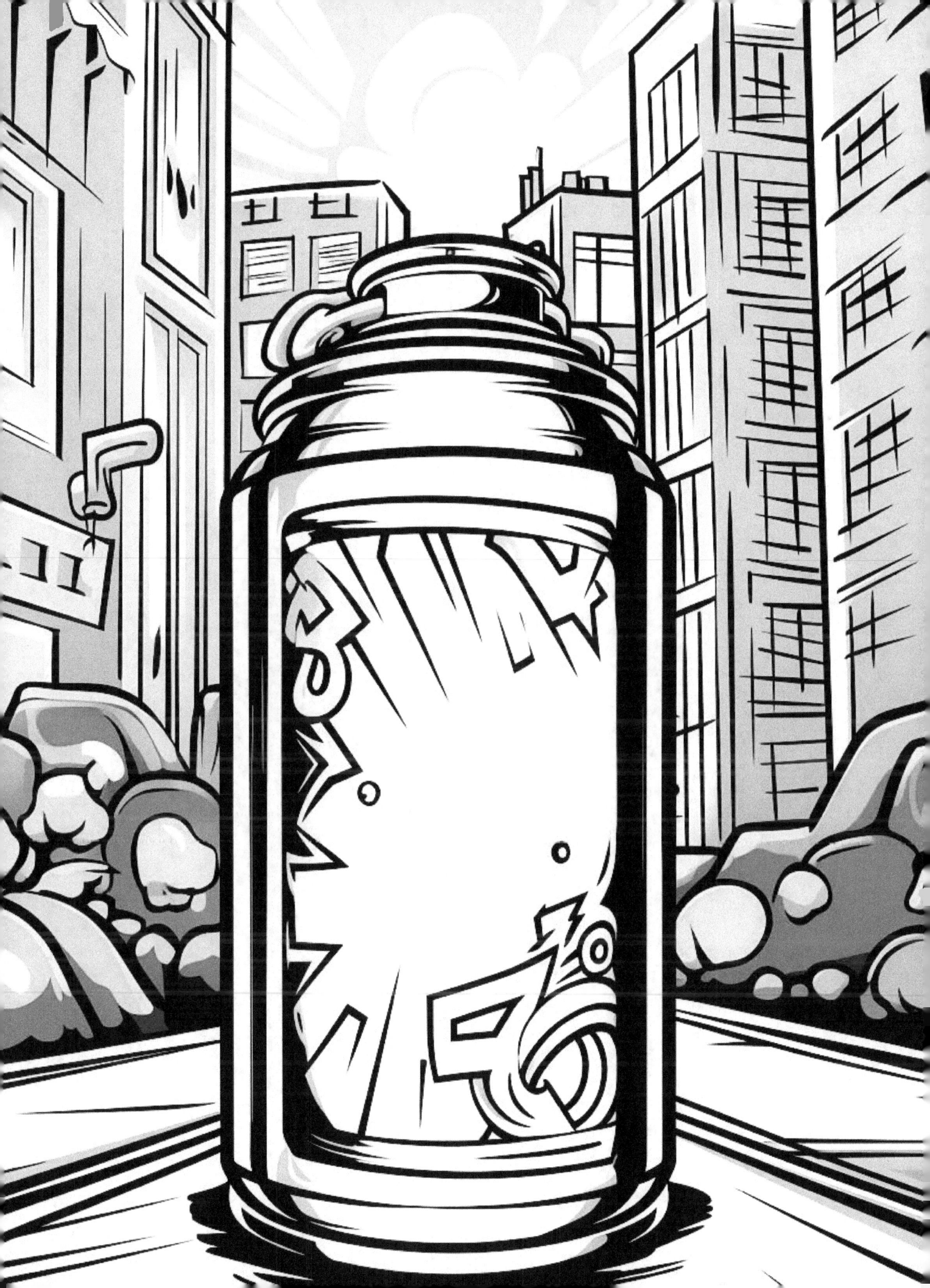

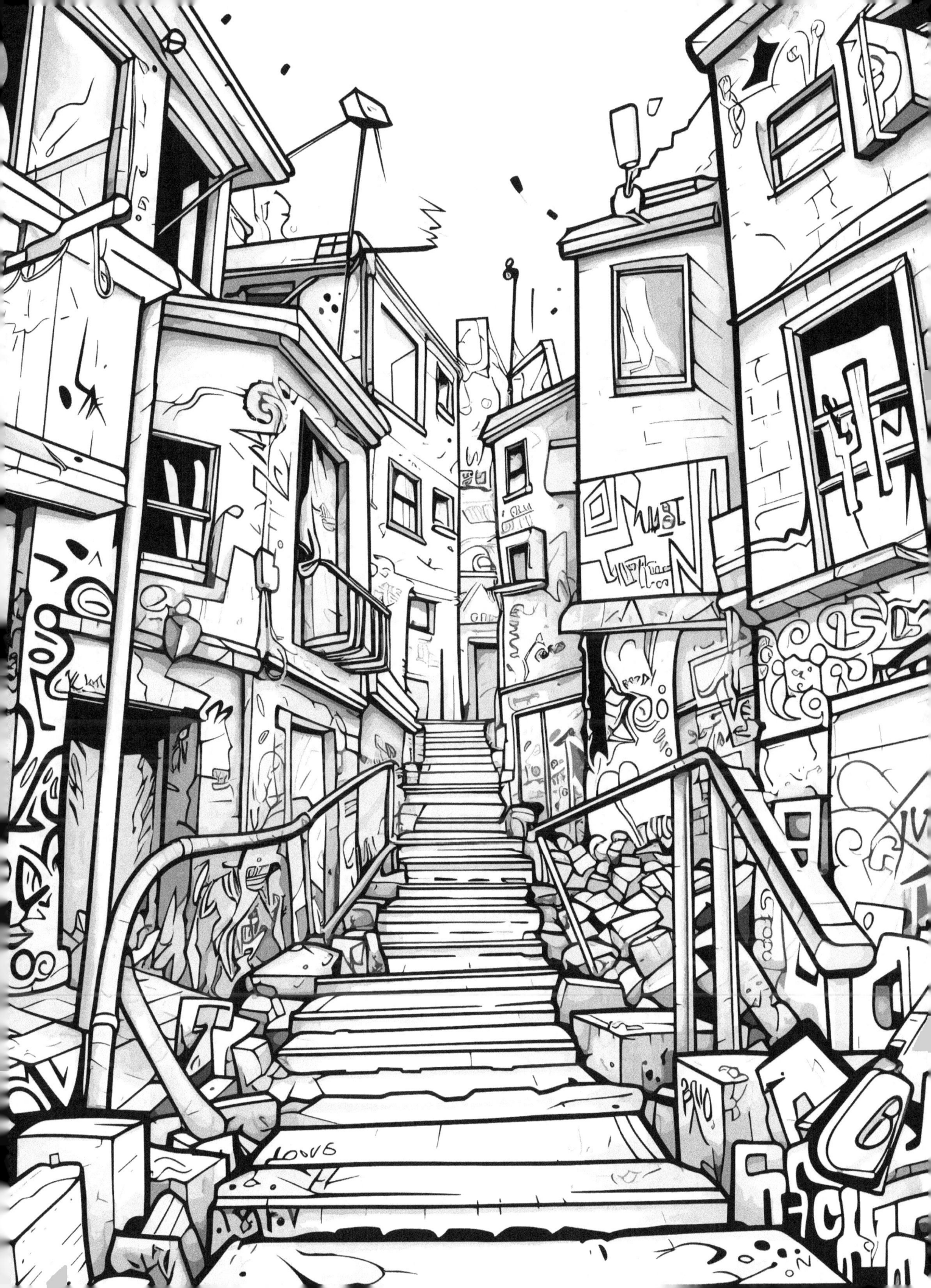

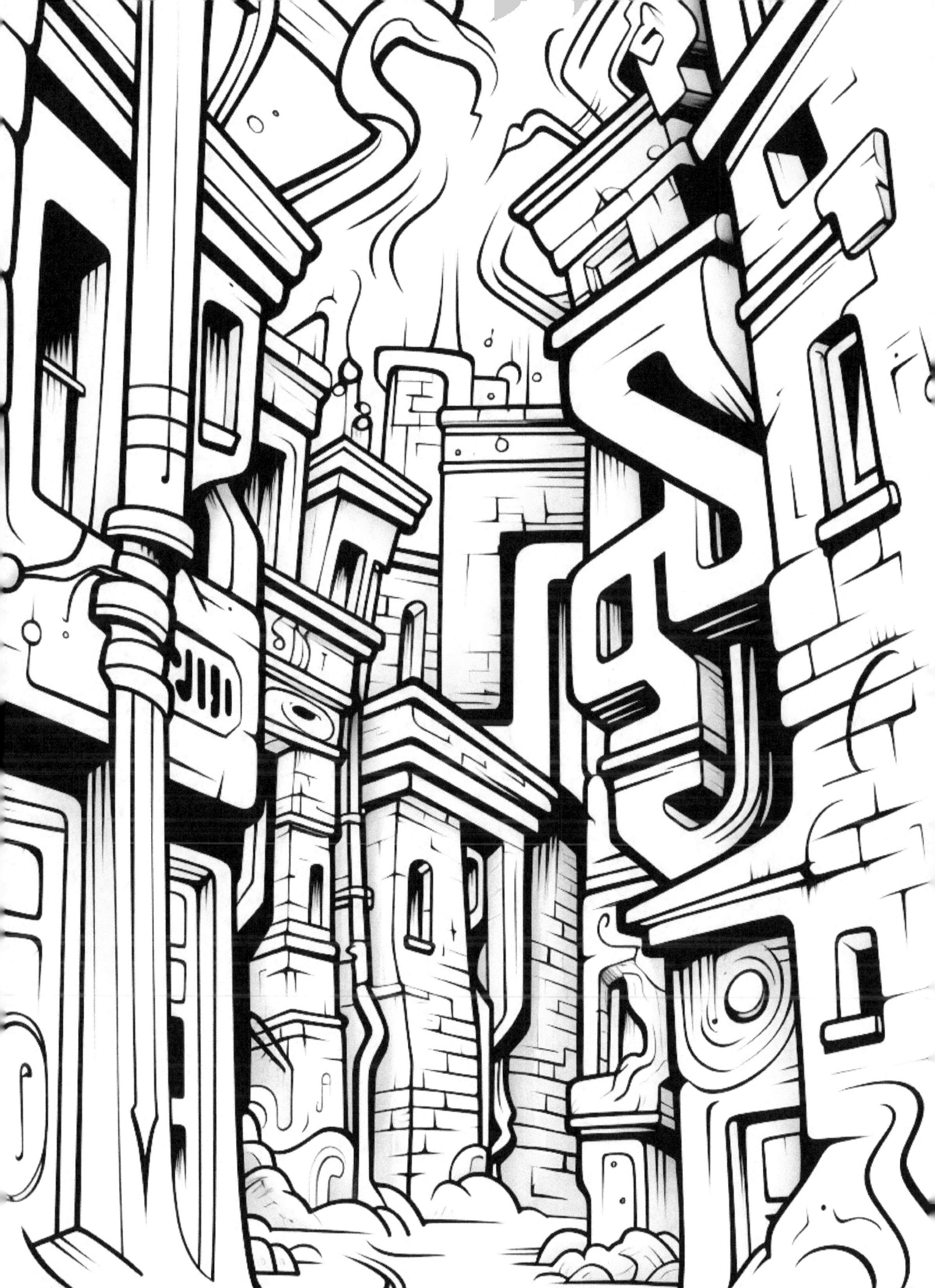

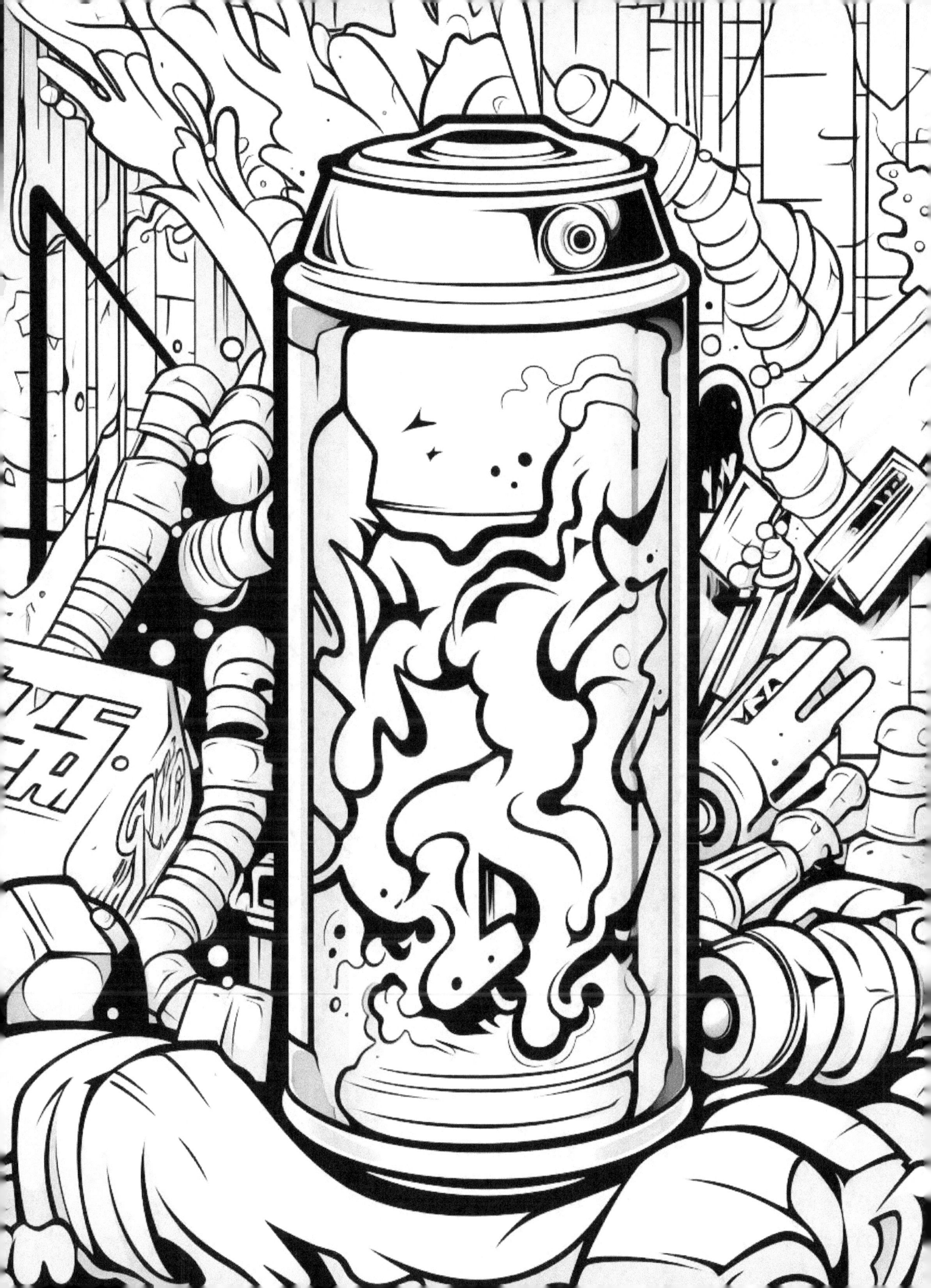

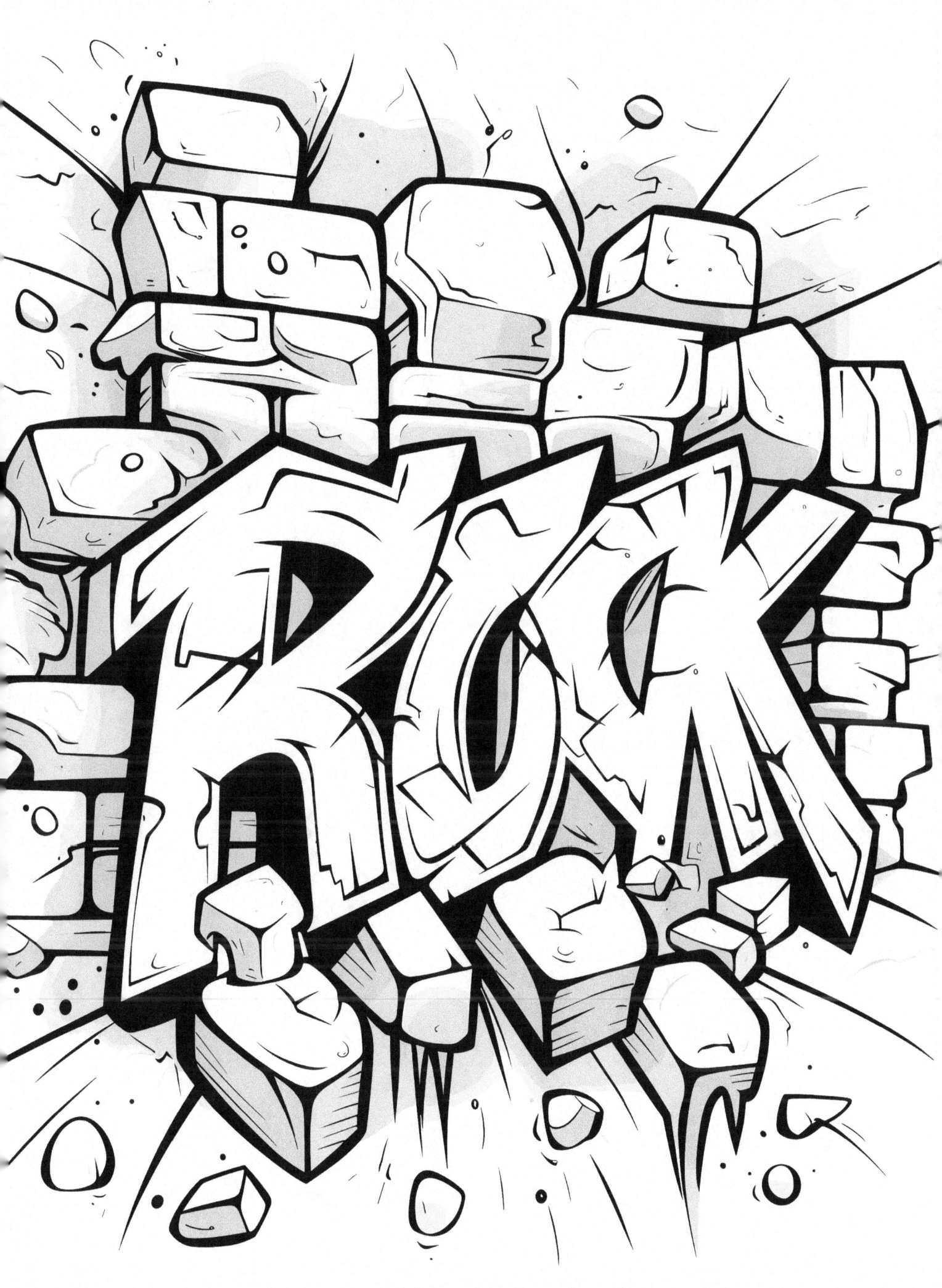

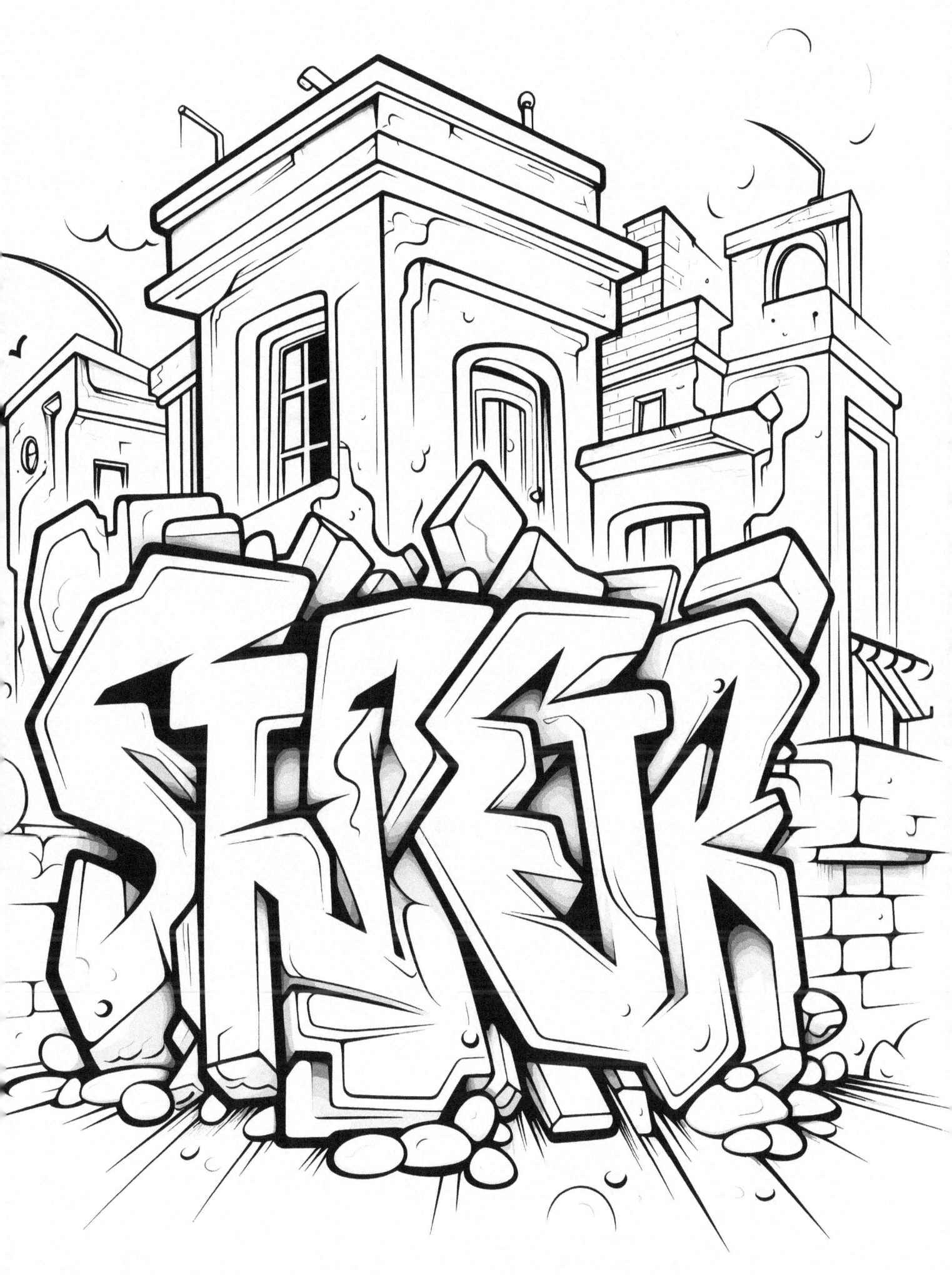

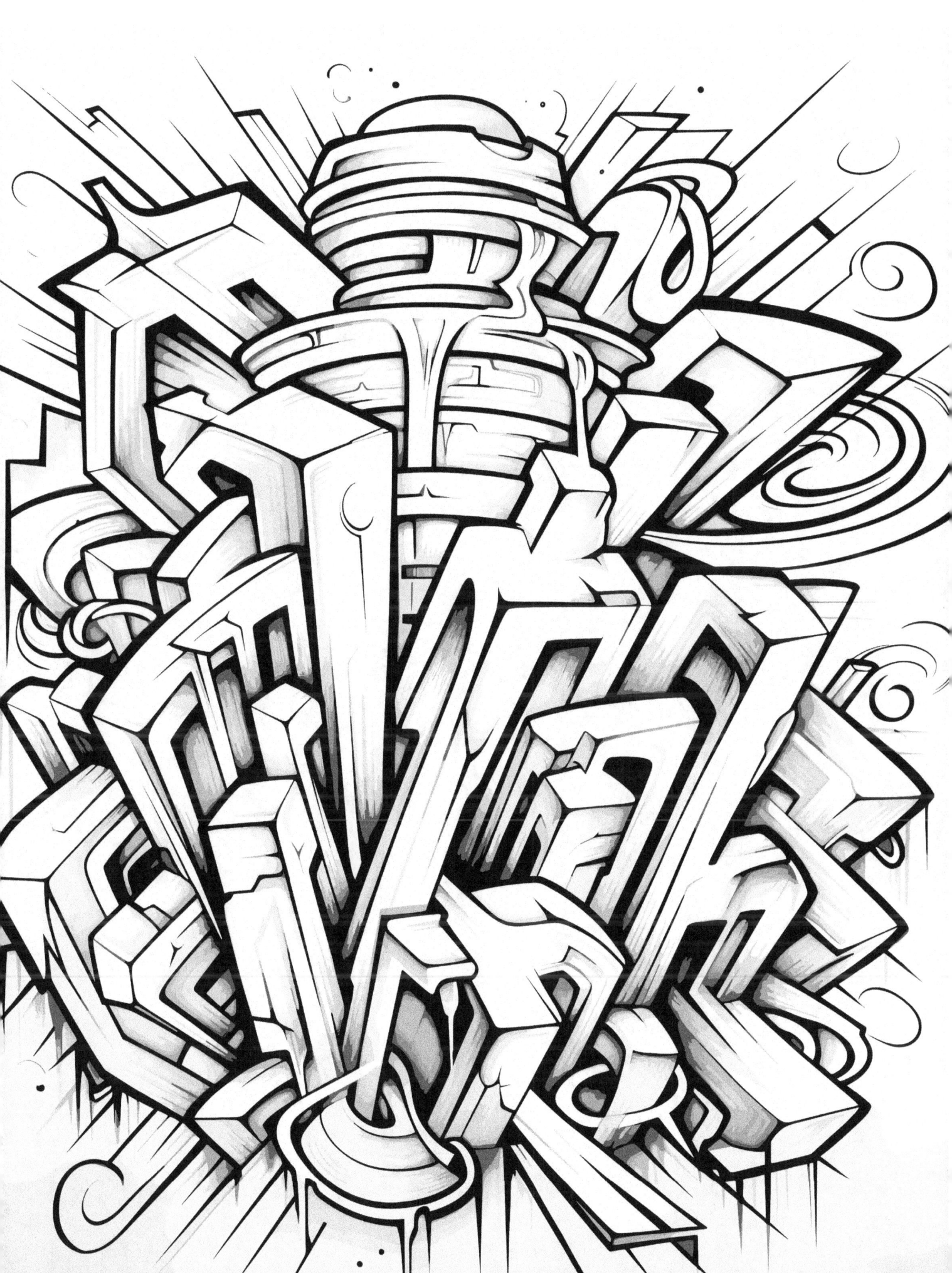

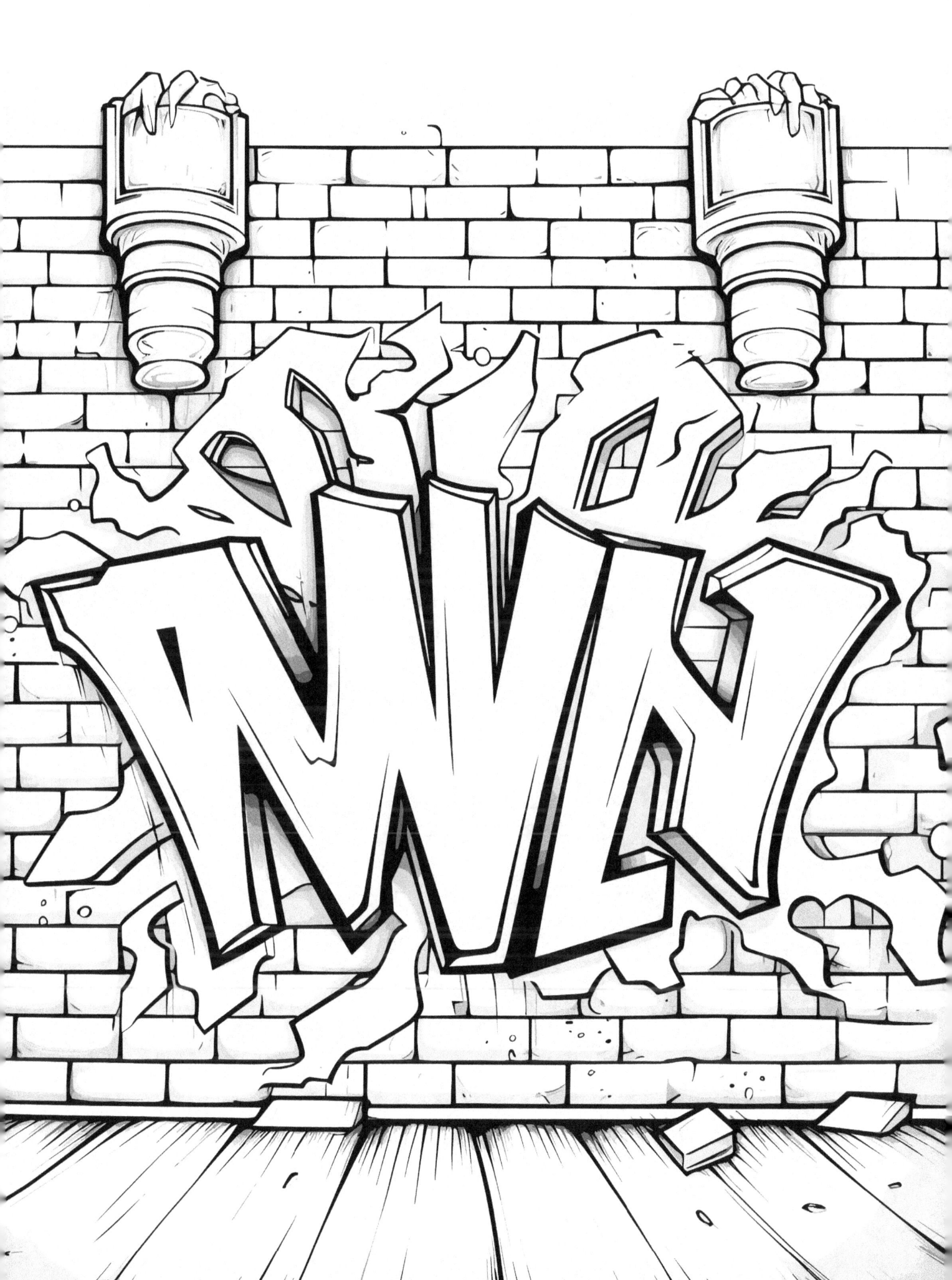

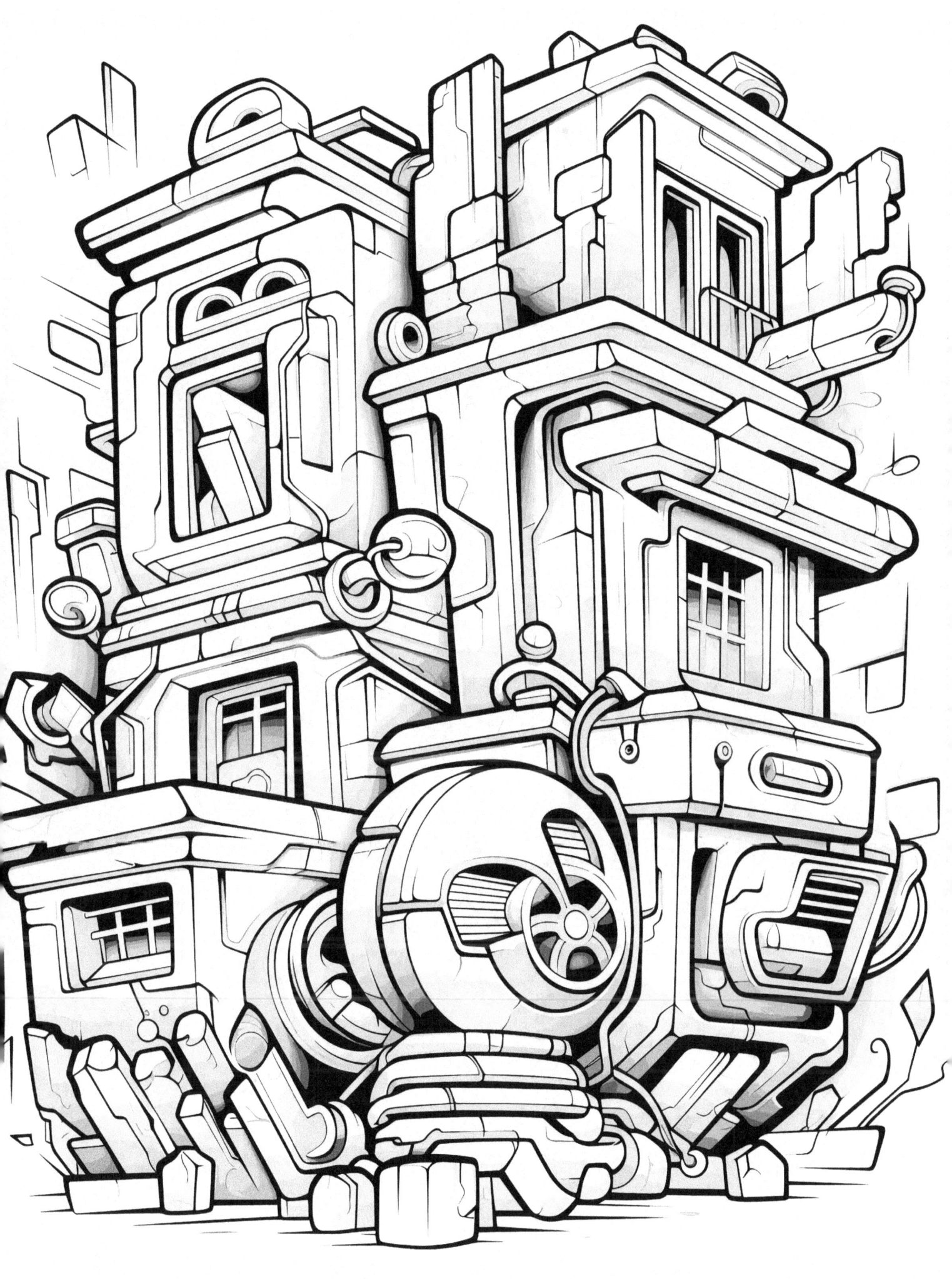

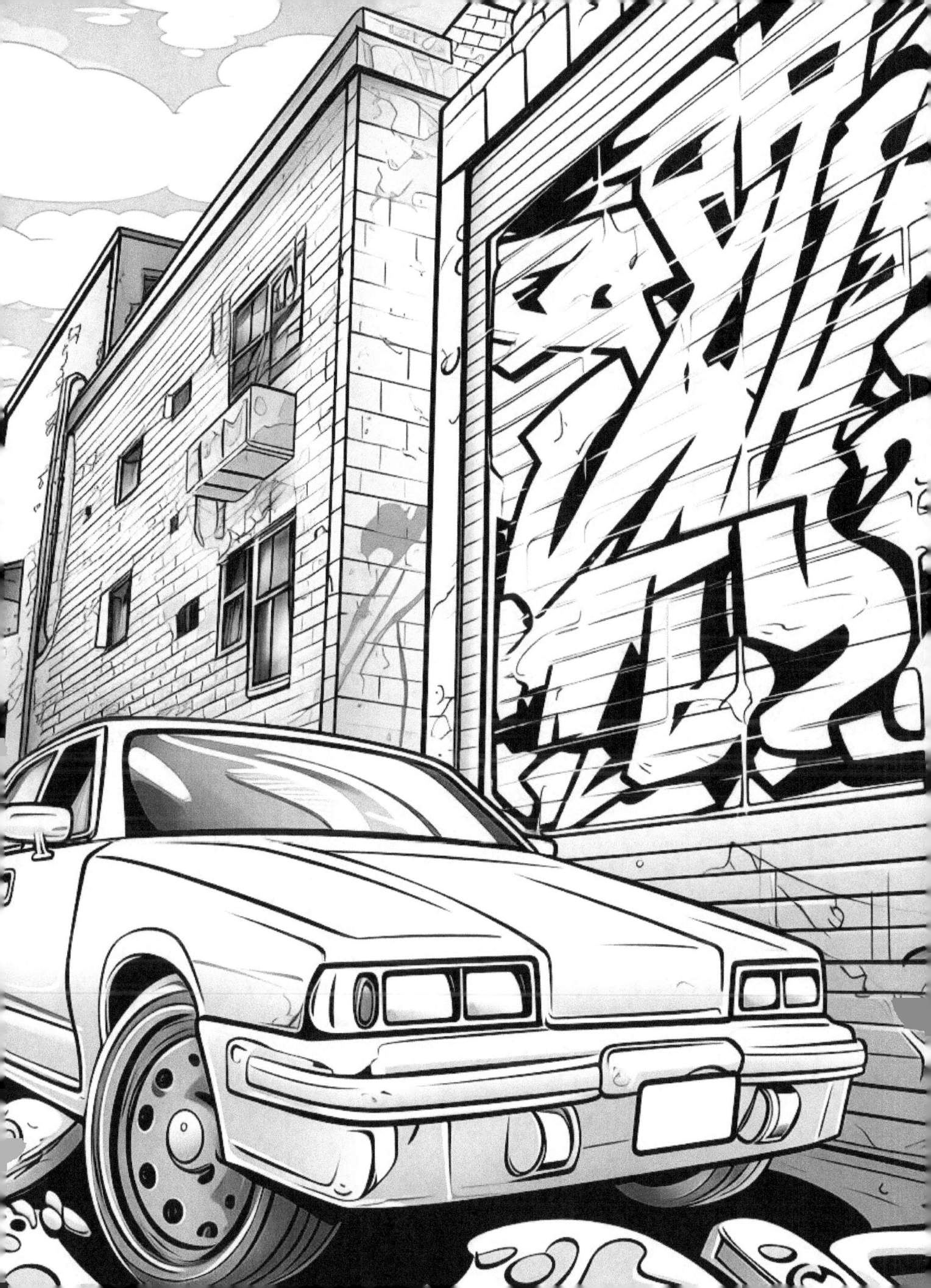

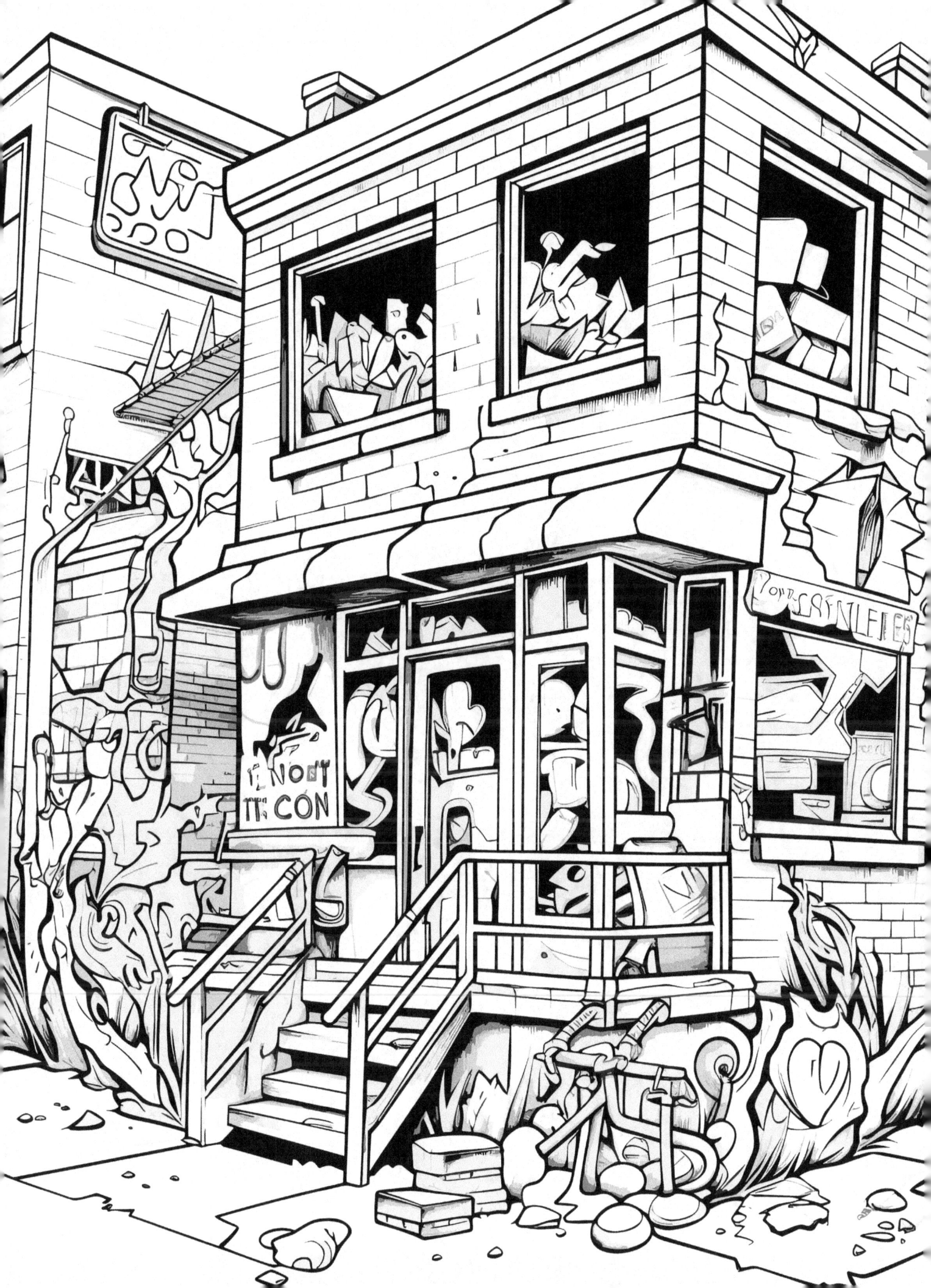

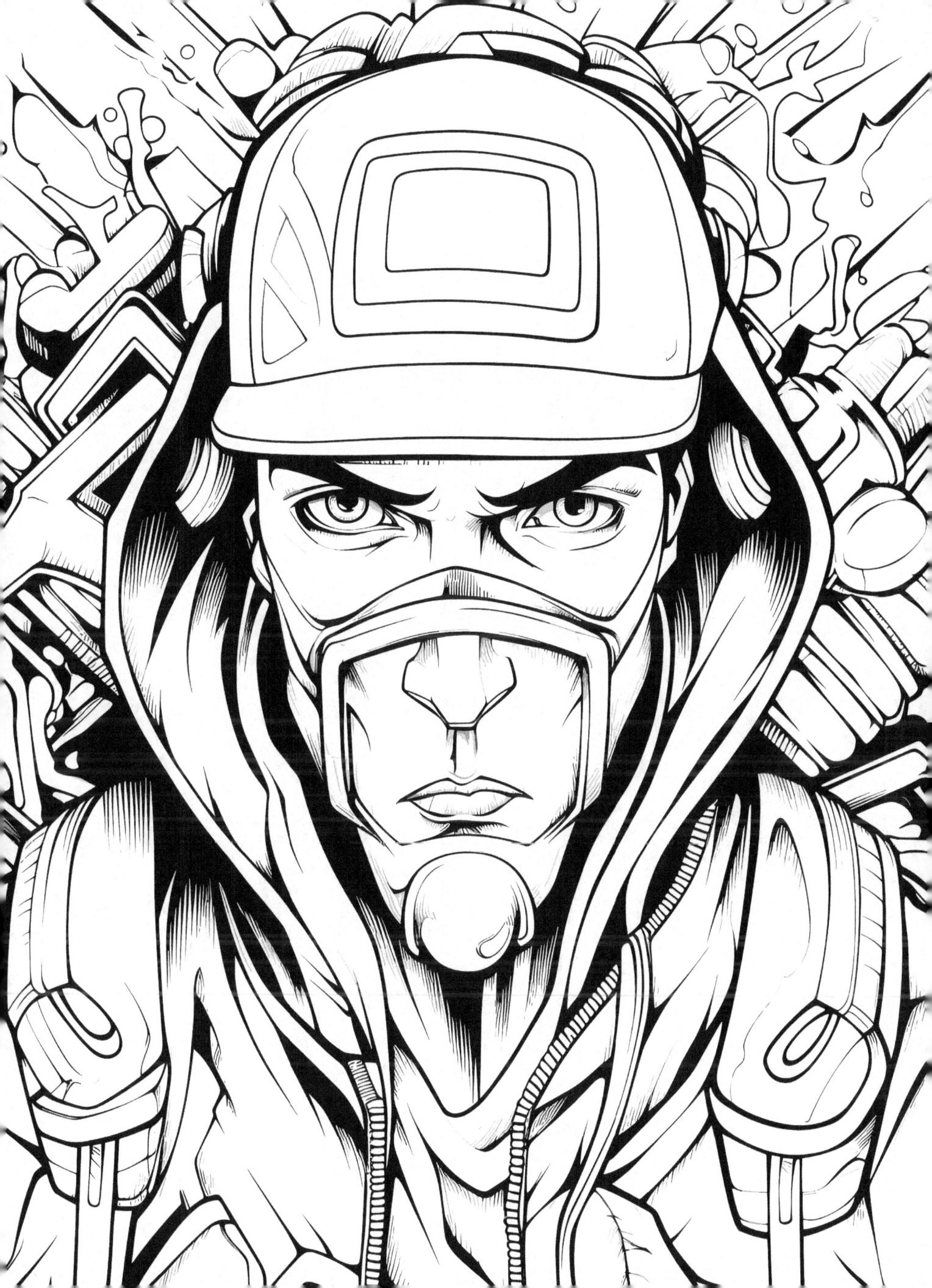

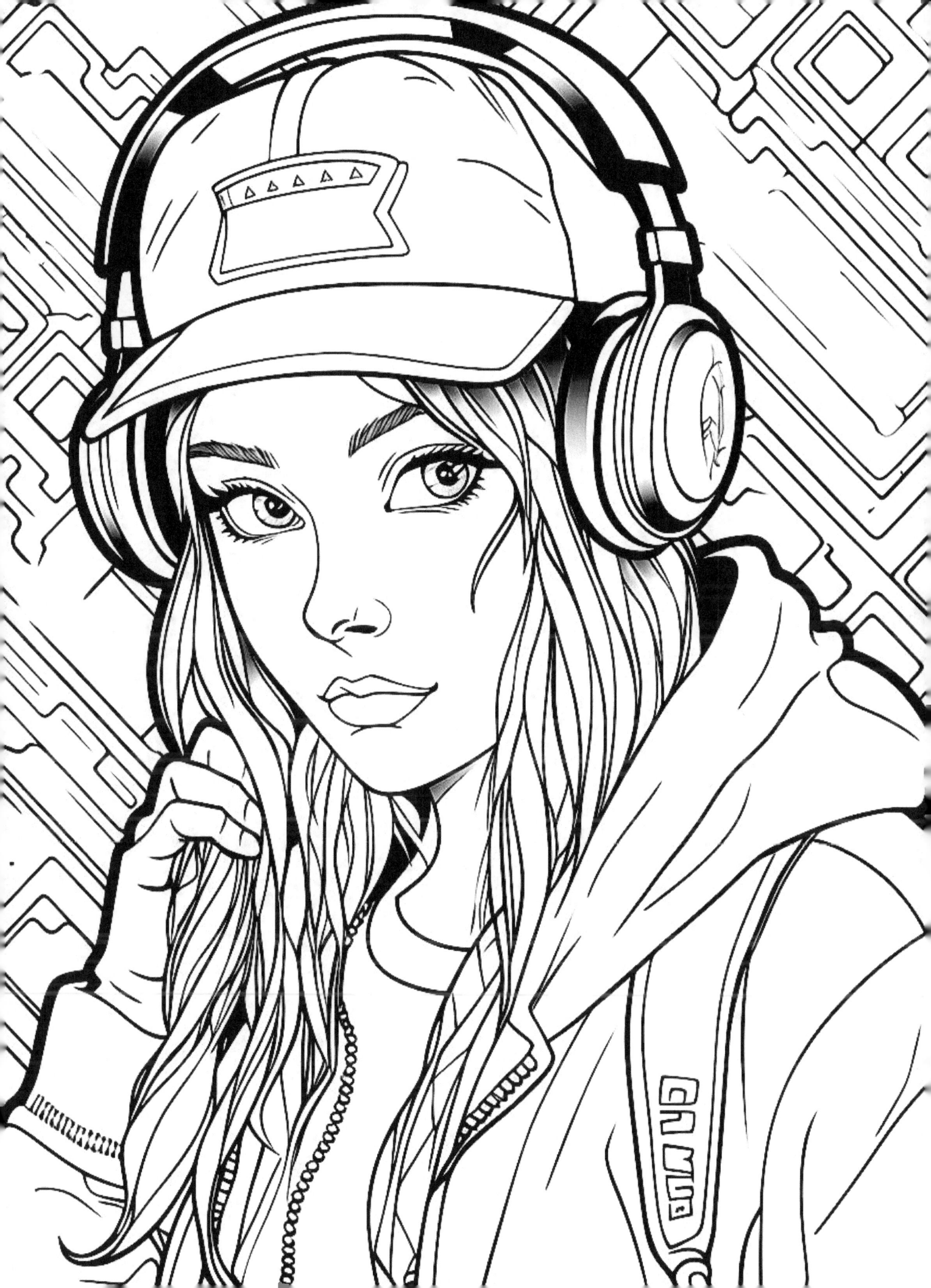

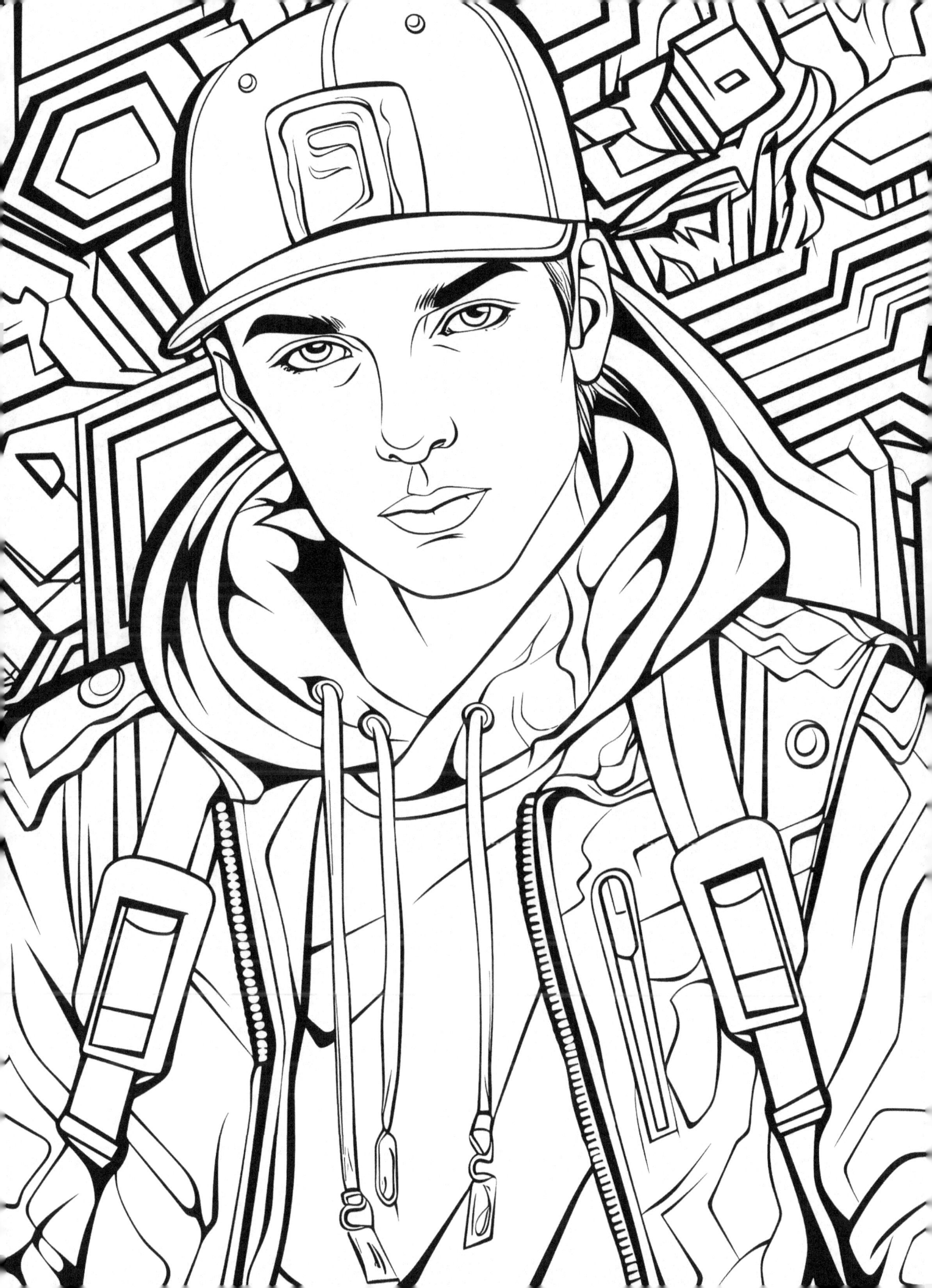

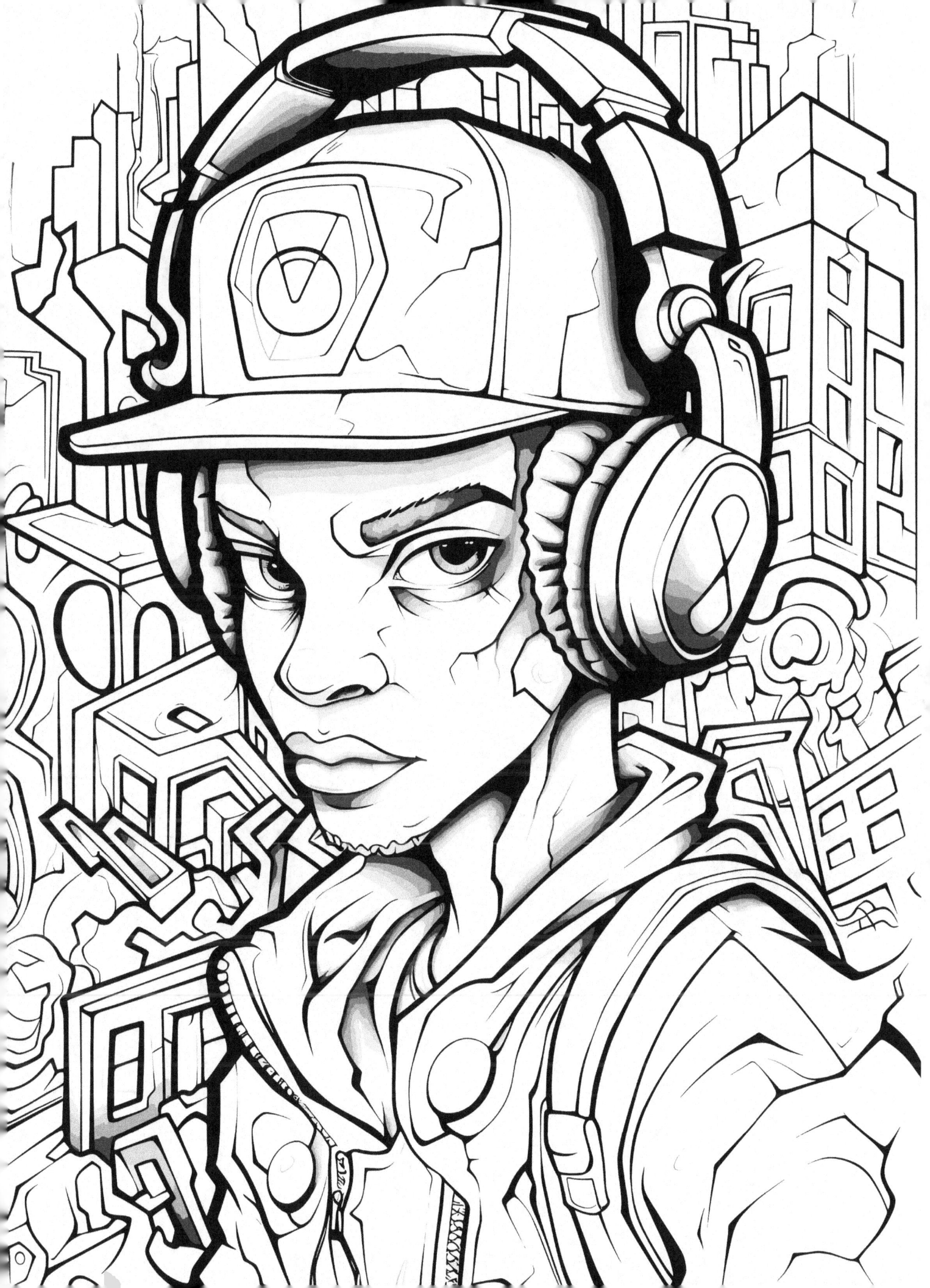

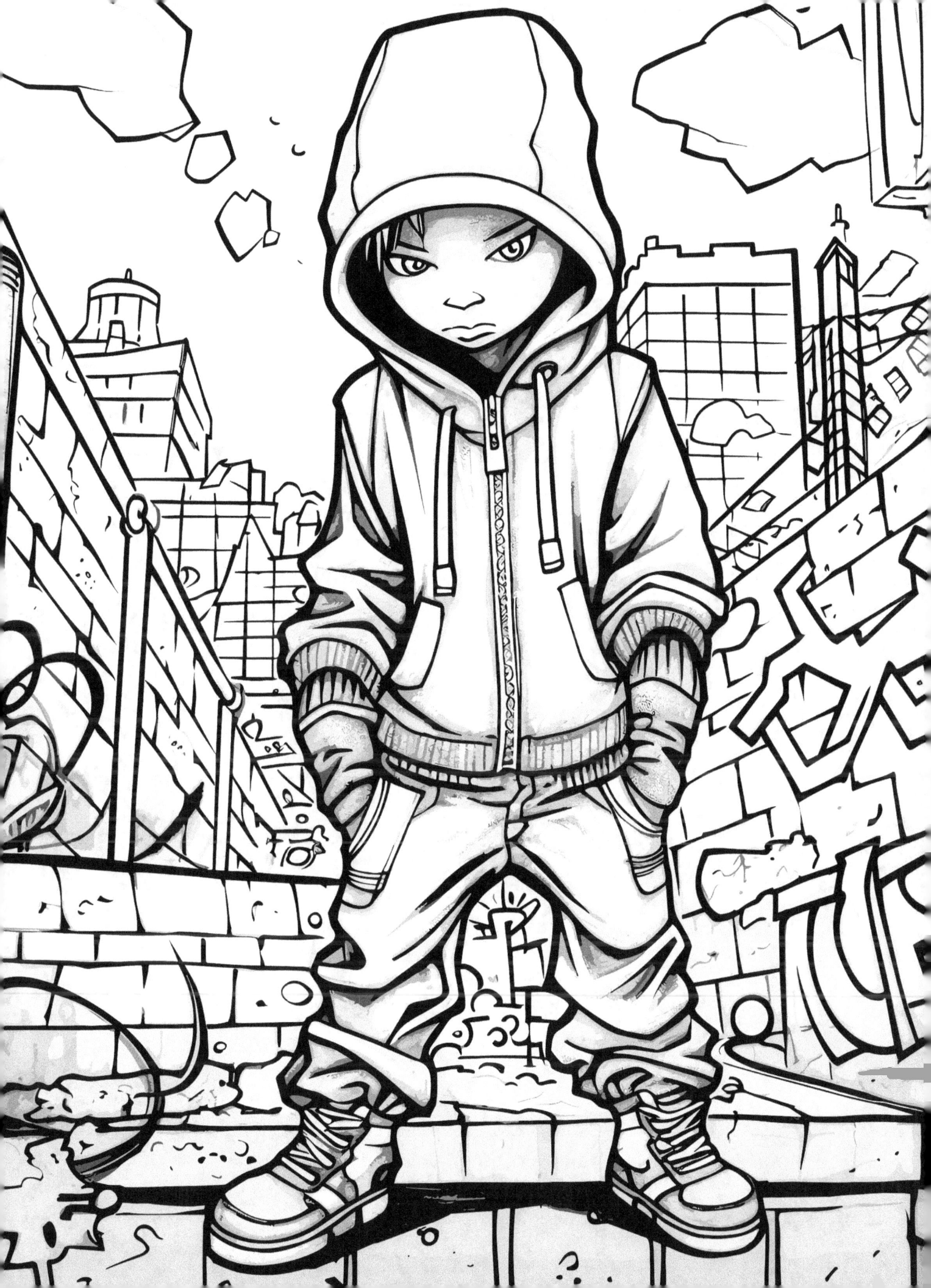

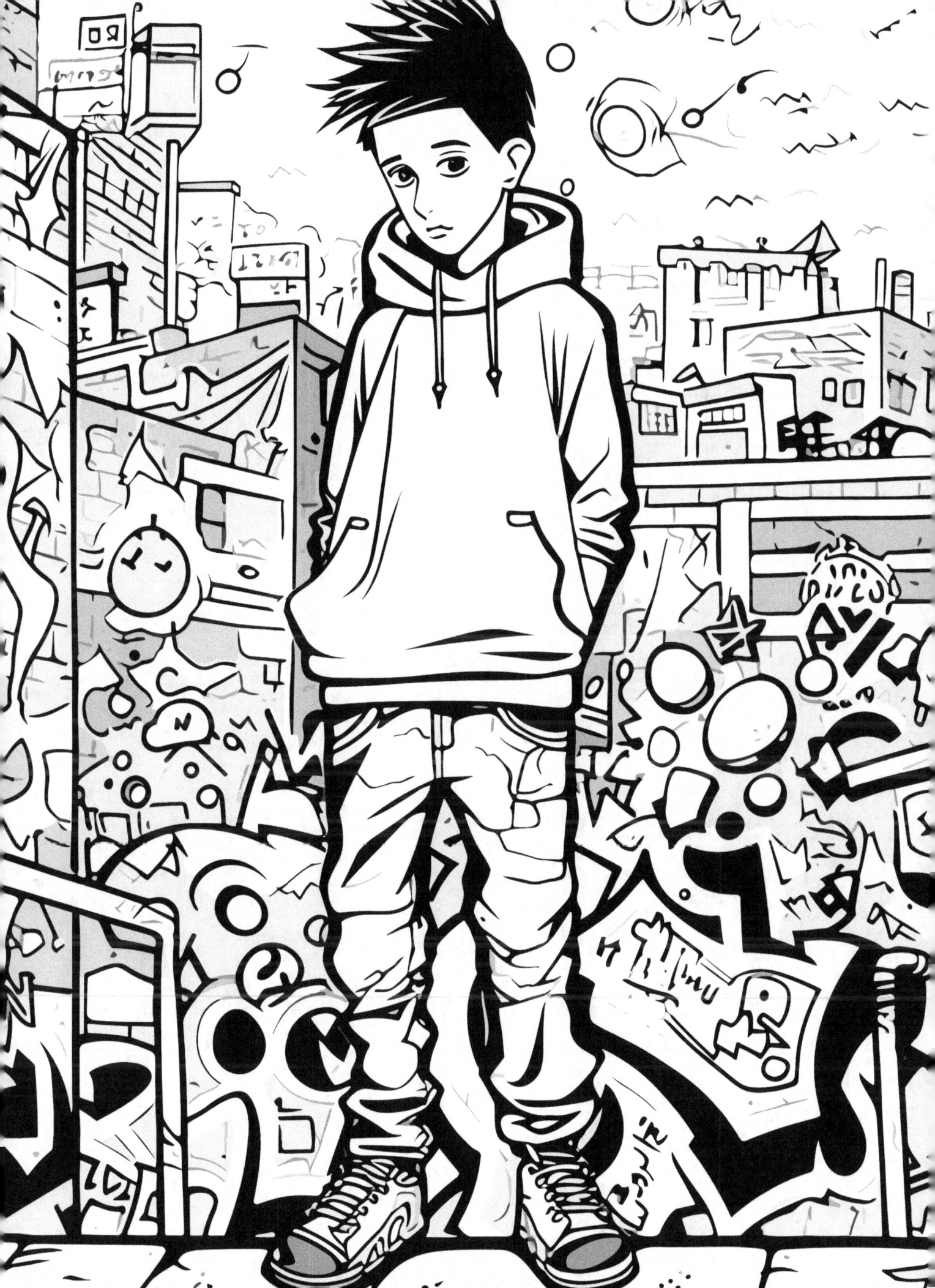

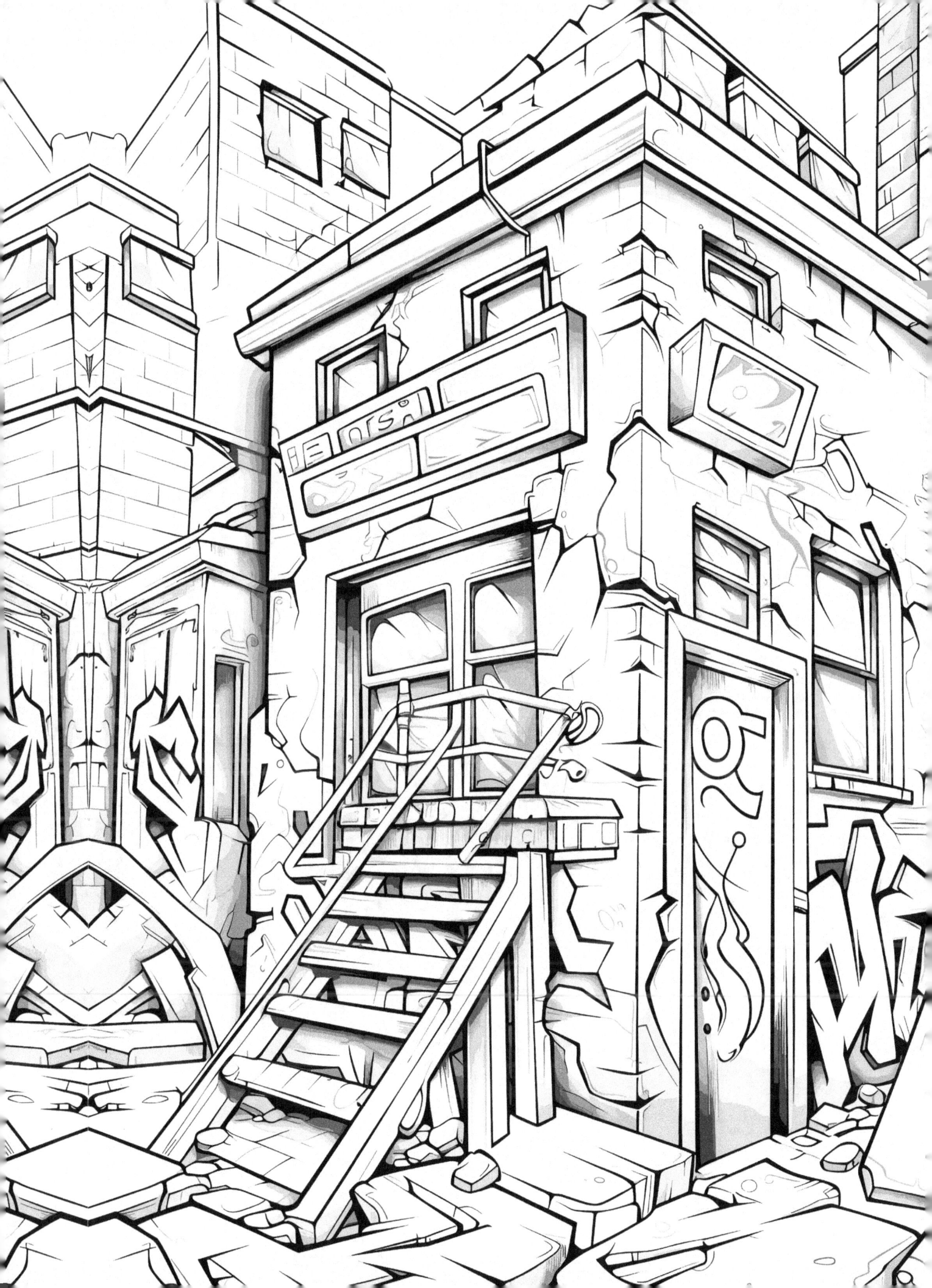

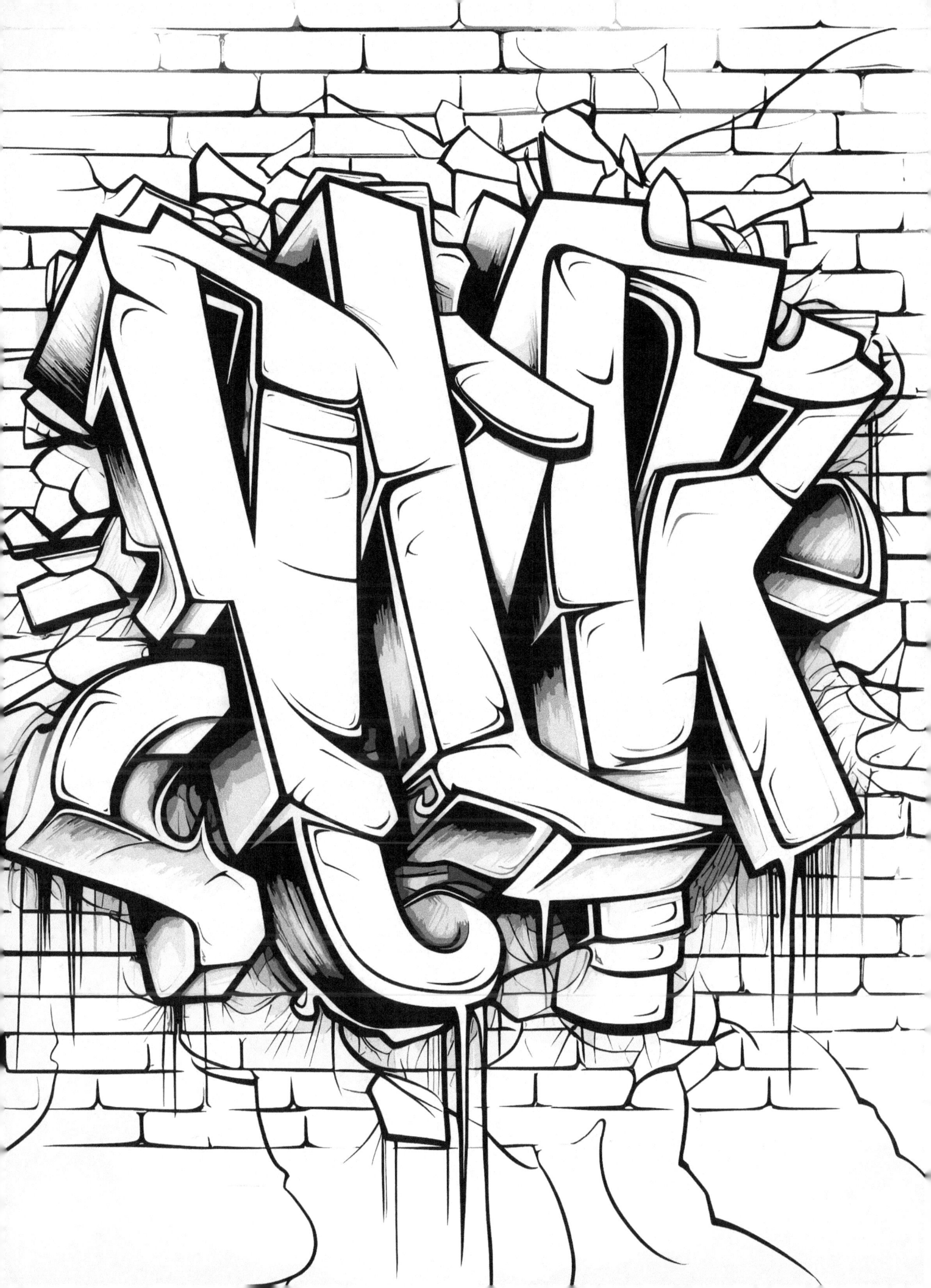

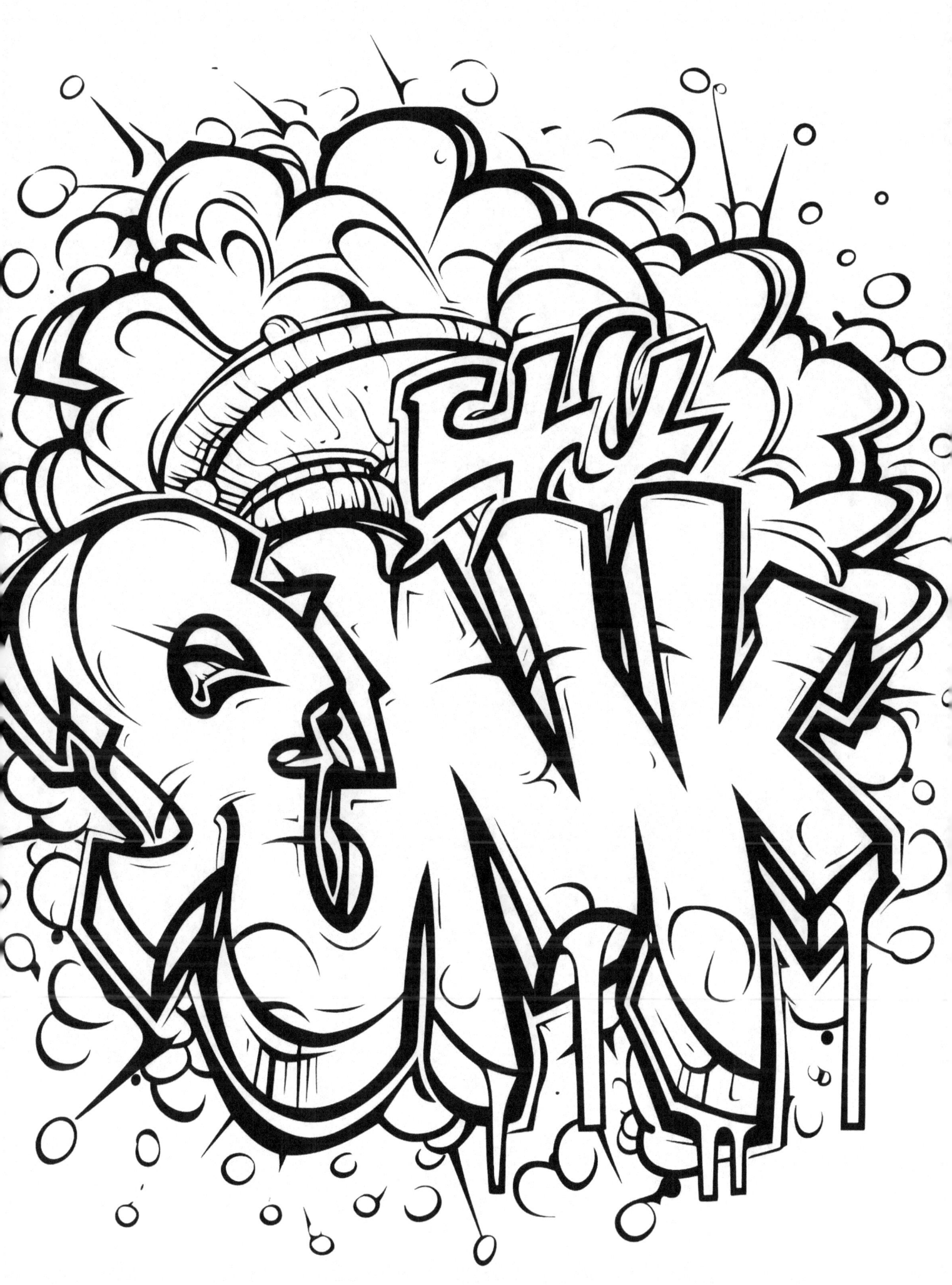

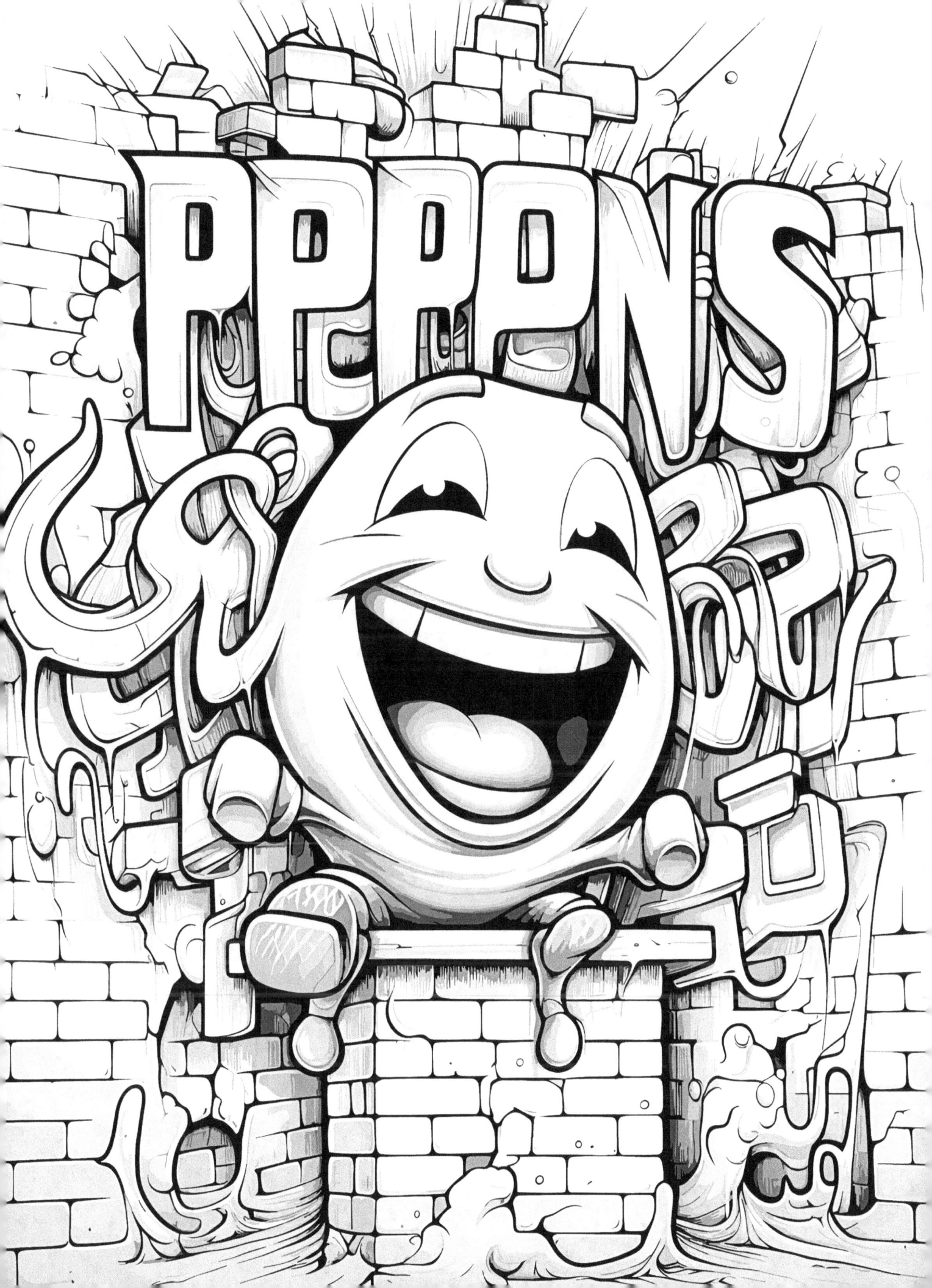

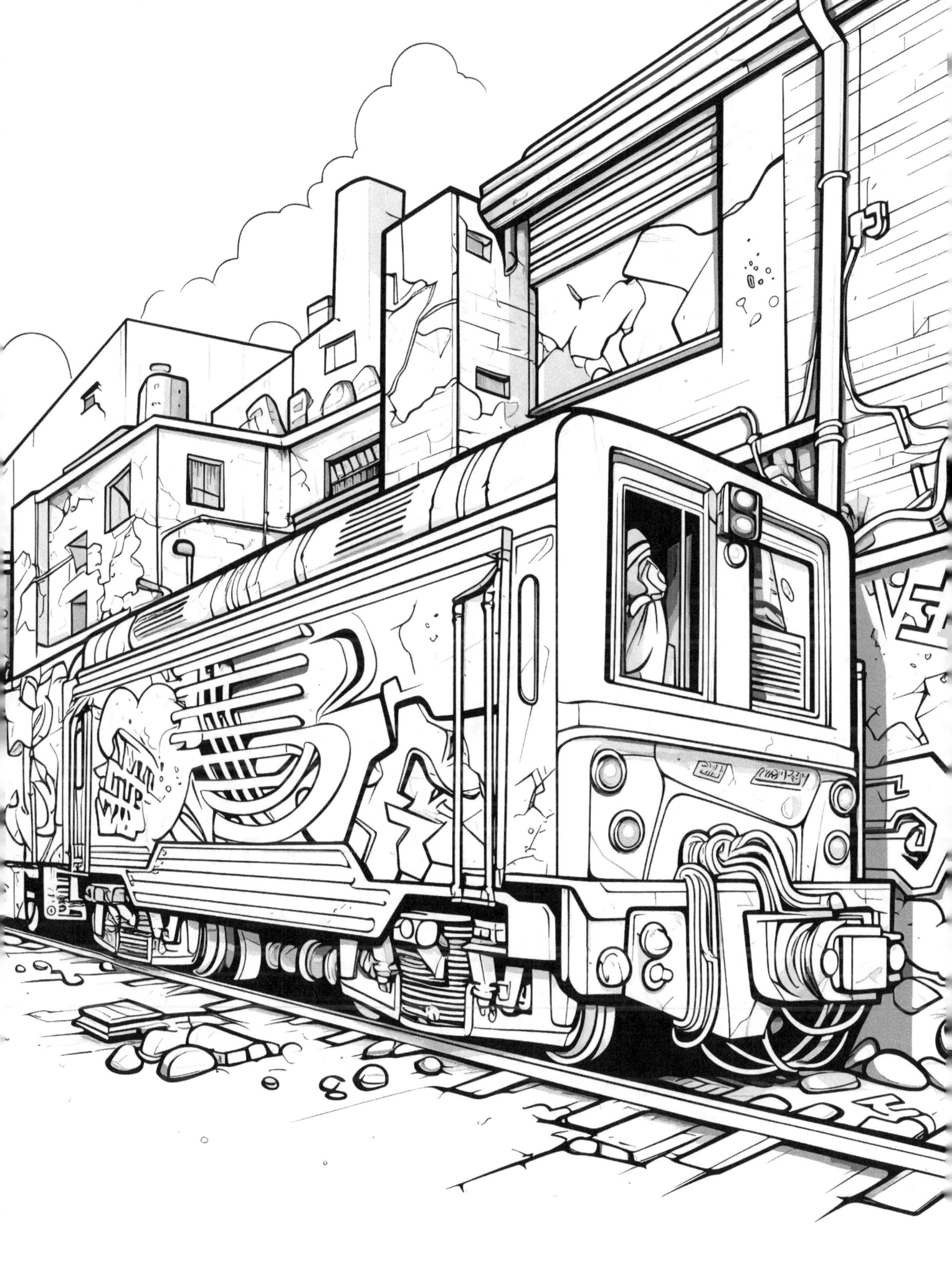

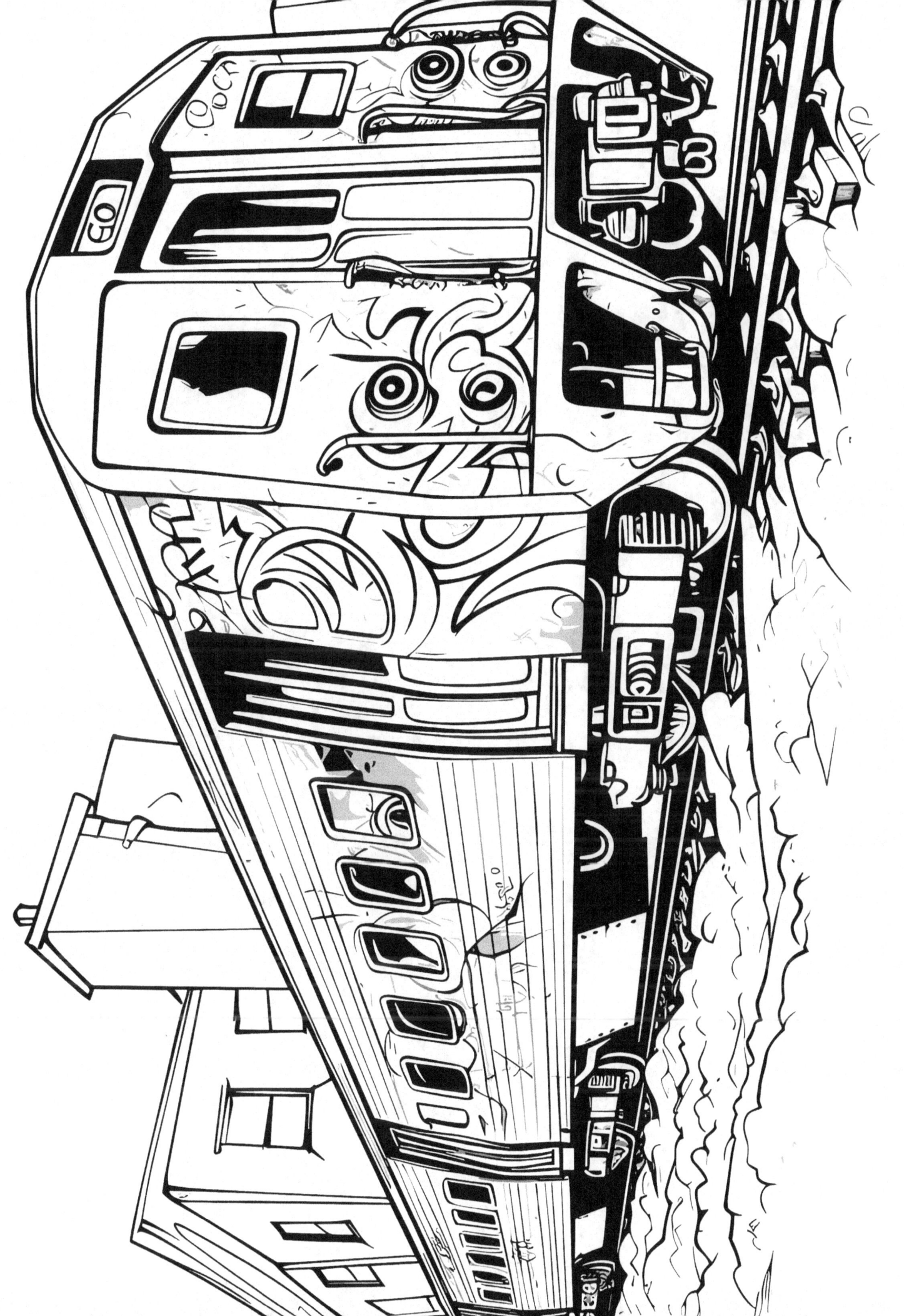

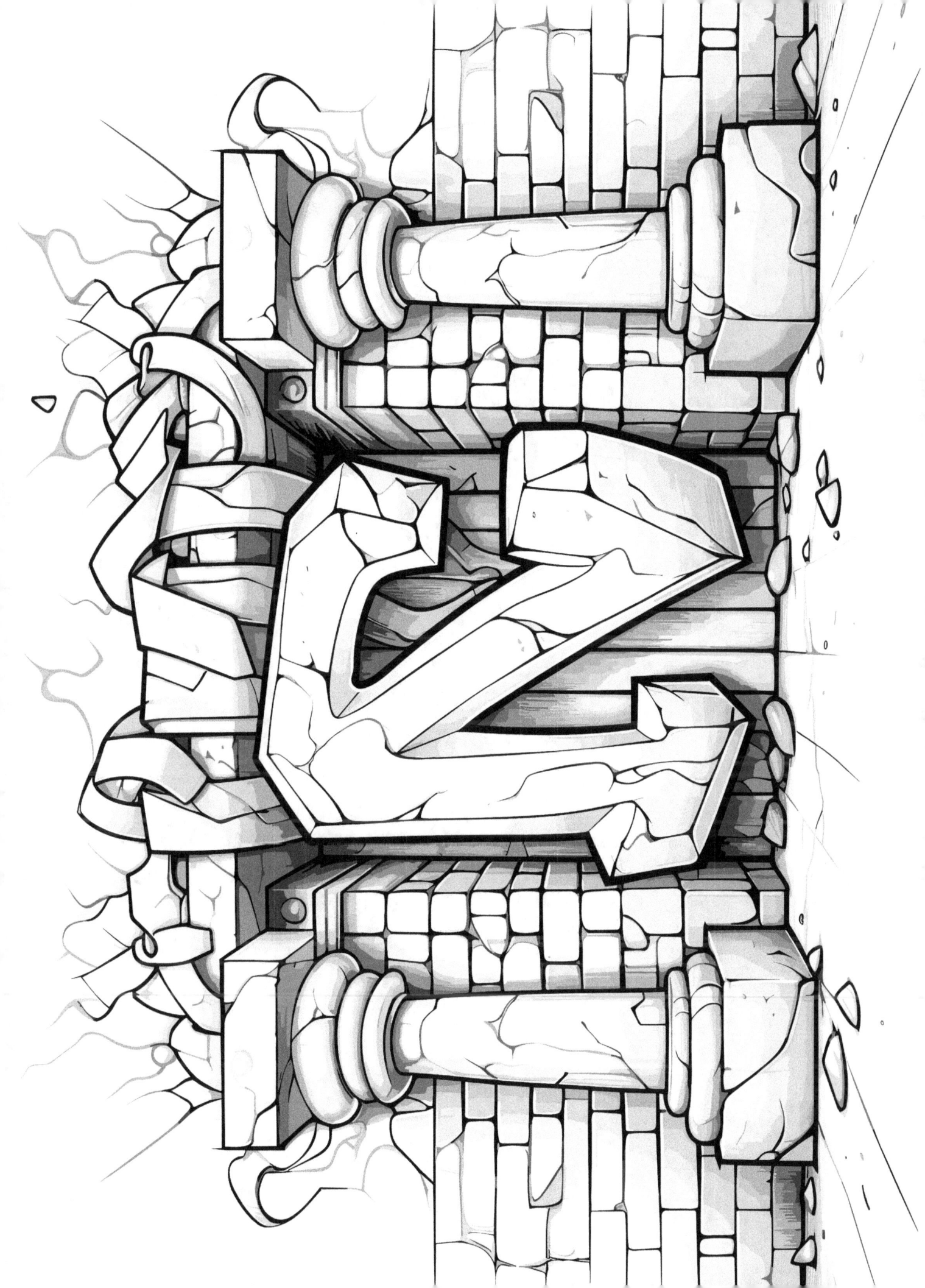

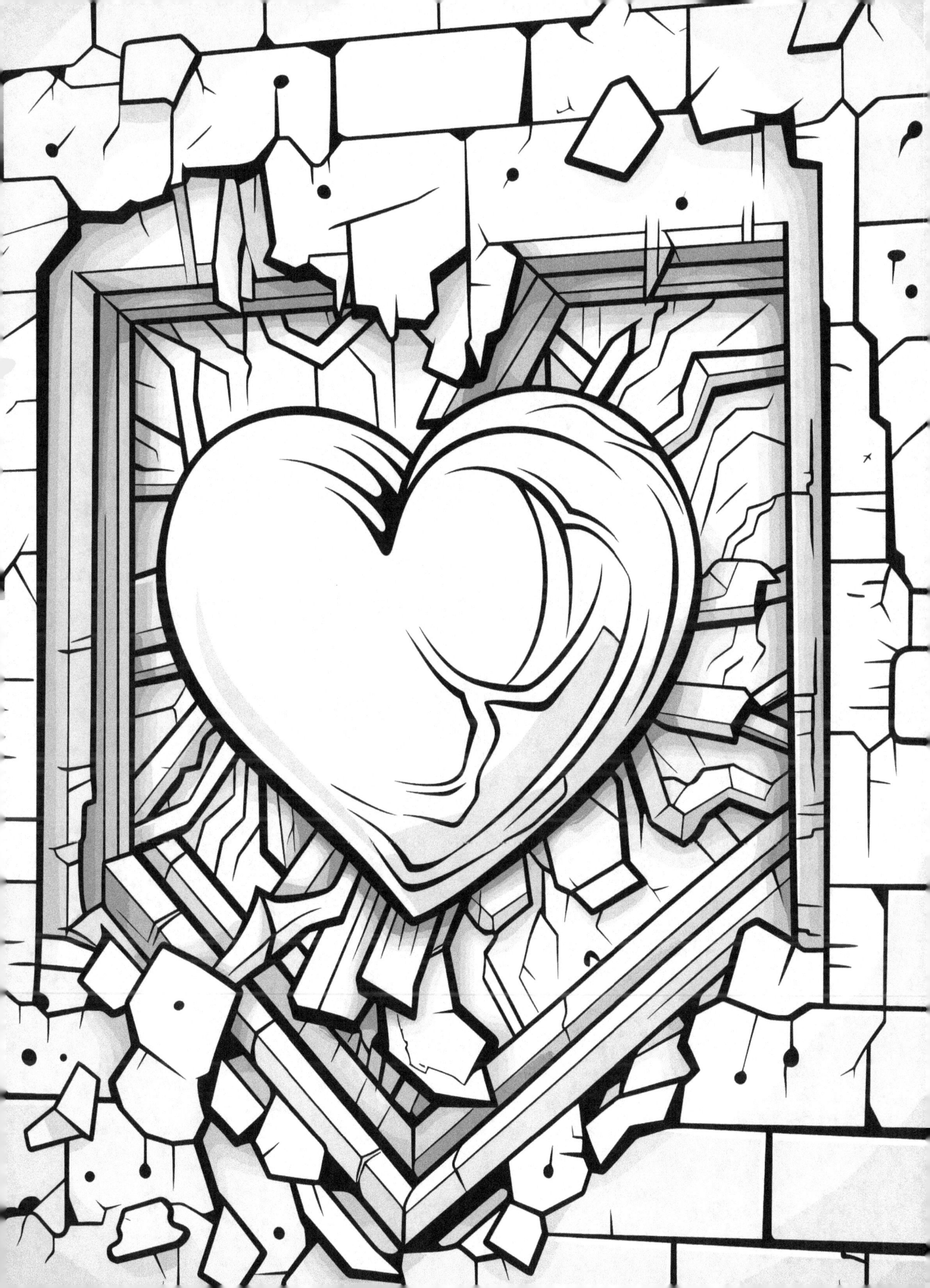

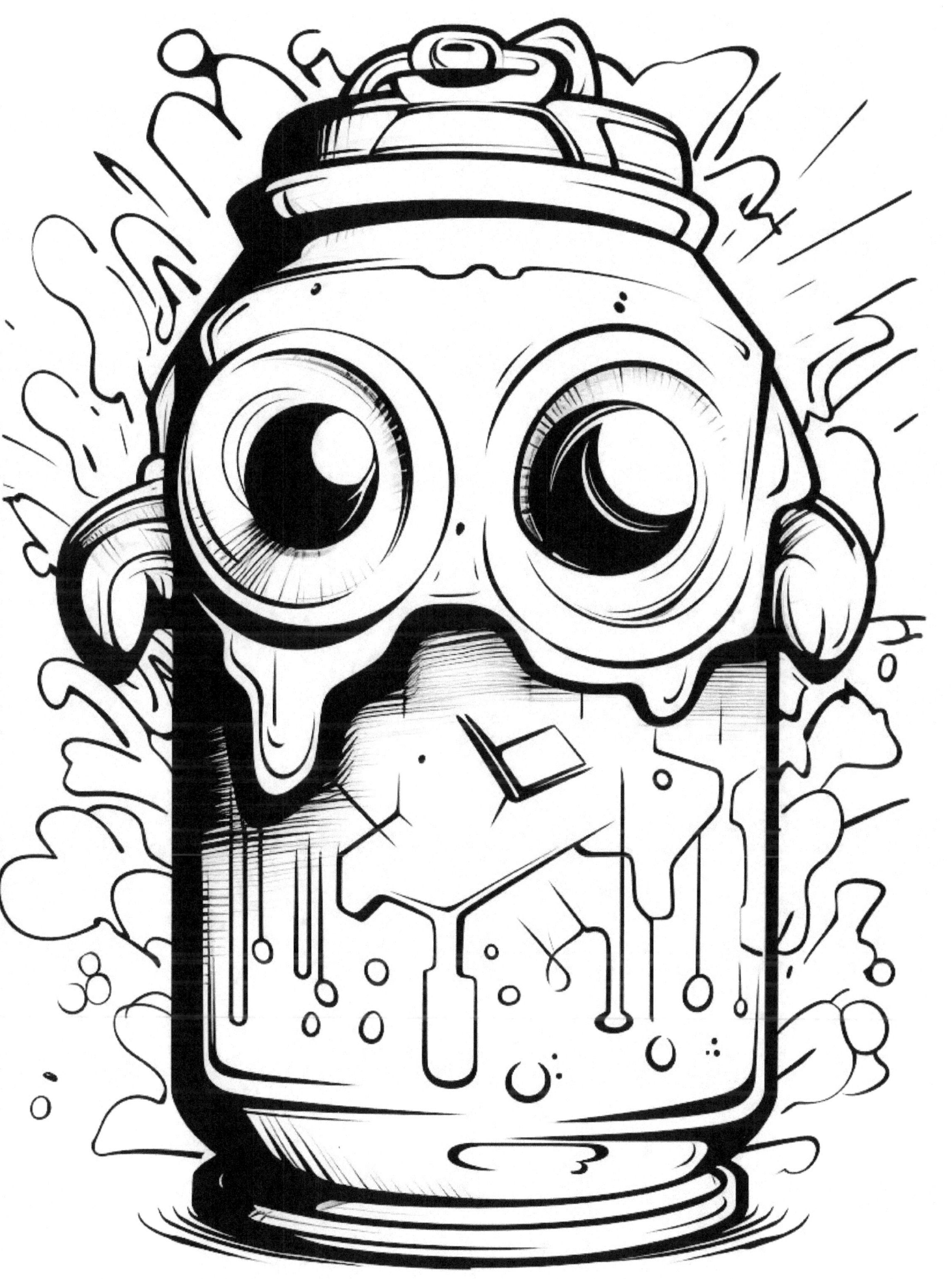

THANK YOU FOR CHOOSING THIS BOOK.

I hope you have enjoyed this book as much as I enjoyed creating it.

Your feedback is very important to me.

If you have encountered any issue with your book, such as printing errors, faulty binding, paper bleeding or any other issue, please do not hesitate to contact me at:

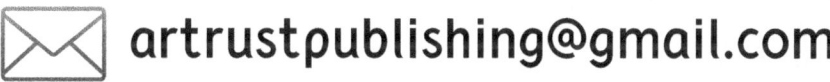 **artrustpublishing@gmail.com**

If you enjoyed this book, please consider leaving a review on the website. It takes a few minutes, but it would be so much appreciated. Reviews are a brilliant thing for small businesses like us – they are the best way to let other potential customers know about the book and your opinion about it.

We encourage you to feel free to add photos of the interior and cover of this book in your review.

Thank you!